Crazy Horse
and
The Coal Man

*For Larry —
Best Wishes —
Roy Baunton*

Crazy Horse
and
The Coal Man

A Memoir

Roy Bainton

©2010 Roy Bainton

The right of Roy Bainton to be identified
as the author of this work has been asserted by him in accordance with
The Copyright, Designs and Patents Act, 1988.

All rights reserved. This book is sold subject to the condition
that it shall not, by way of trade or otherwise, be lent, re-sold,
hired out or otherwise circulated in any form of binding or cover
other than that in which it is published and without a similar
condition including this condition being imposed
on the subsequent purchaser.

A copy of the British Library Cataloguing in
Publication Data is available from the British Library.

ISBN 978-1-4461-9727-1

Published, Printed and bound in the UK
by www.lulu.com

*For Dave and Carol Iles,
and my family.*

*We cherish our friends,
not for their ability to amuse us,
but for our ability to amuse them.*

Other works by Roy Bainton

Talk To Me Baby,
The Story of The Blues Band,
(Firebird Books, Dorset 1994)
Honoured By Strangers,
The Life of Capt. F.N.A. Cromie RN 1882-1918
(Airlife/Crowood Press, 2002)
The Long Patrol:
The British in Germany since 1945
(Mainstream, Edinburgh, 2003)
A Brief History of 1917:
Russia's Year of Revolution
(Constable & Robinson, London 2005)
The Alternative Mansfield Brew:
A Worker's History of Mansfield Brewery
(EMc Press Ltd. Mansfield 2006)
Iron In The Blood
(Co-authored with Kevin Fegan)
(Artery, Derbyshire, 2007)
The Scrap Run
(EMc Press Ltd. Mansfield 2008) written
with the generous aid of a Literature Grant
from Arts Council England East Midlands
Slightly Out of Tune
(Co-authored with Norman Wattam)
EMc Press Ltd. Mansfield 2009
Tiger Heart, Velvet Paw
EMc Press Ltd. Mansfield 2009

www.roybaintonwrites.com

PREFACE

Contrary to his numerous appearances in the following text, this isn't a biography of the great Lakota Sioux chief, Tsunke Witco, a.k.a. Crazy Horse, and the eponymous coal man only occupies a necessary cameo role. This is simply the nostalgic, light hearted story of a Yorkshire boy's family life up to the age of thirteen, of growing up in poverty in Hull, Halifax and on the East Yorkshire coast. During those formative years, Crazy Horse was, and remains, sixty years later, his inspiration and his spiritual anchor. My period as a Plains Indian was at its maximum intensity between the ages of eight to twelve. After that, I saw myself as an amalgam of Elvis Presley, Chuck Berry and latterly Herman Melville's Ishmael in *Moby Dick*. But as alter-egos go, Crazy Horse has always been the noblest and the best.

After well over half a century, I'll have to apologise in advance if my topographic memory plays any tricks. The map of 21st century Hull is barely recognisable alongside that of 1945. Also, there are numerous characters mentioned, some related, others friends. Many will be long dead, others, like me, might be still around, loitering in God's waiting room. Thus, in order to protect the innocent, some names have been changed.

Like other Native American Nations, the Sioux, cheated, attacked, lied to, removed from their lands, victims of genocide from the day the first white men appeared on their territory, rightly have little time for romantic white men 'pretending' to be 'Indians.' There are people, here in Britain, who think it cool to spend a 'New Age' holiday in the Welsh hills, (and even in Yorkshire) living in a tipi and wearing buckskins as they sit around a wood fire beating drums. It may be harmless 'fun' yet it simply skims the thin top layer off a culture of such rich and unfathomable depth and turns it into nothing less than cheap, gift-shop 'native' jewellery.

Hollywood has a lot to answer for, too. Tinsel town's portrayal of the Native American as a violent, scalp-taking beast, played by a procession of pan-caked Caucasian stars from Victor Mature's abysmal *Crazy Horse* in 1954 (alternative title *Valley of Fury*) to a Bronx-accented *Geronimo* played by Chuck Connors in 1962 tells us little of the tragedy which befell them in the years after the massacre at Wounded Knee in 1890. Even the award-winning Dances *with Wolves* succumbed to the old Western cliché – Kevin Costner's dalliance with a Native American woman is OK, because she isn't really an Indian – she's a kidnapped white girl. Some amends have been made; we'll skip over John Ford's belated sackcloth and ashes approach to his previous Indian portrayals with his 1966 *Cheyenne Autumn,* but Wes Studi's impressive *Geronimo* in 1993 and HBO's 2007 *Bury My Heart at Wounded Knee* have set new standards.

However, a kid needs heroes, and in the sheer innocence of an immediate post-war English childhood I found mine, in a land well over 3,000 miles from the Black Hills. For Crazy Horse, Yorkshire would have been as alien as the surface of Mars. The possibility of a member of the Lakota Nation reading this little book about a distant, unfamiliar culture seems remote. Yet if you, dear reader, are such a person, please accept my apologies for purloining your heritage in my childhood. It was done with a good heart.

Tiyospaye

The Sioux were a nation whose history of war frequently overshadows their great humanity and compassion, sidelined as it often was by the white man's aggressive and rapacious push westward. Throughout Lakota history, the Sioux's sense of community and family were the cornerstones of their life. This went beyond the boundaries of immediate family, siblings, children and parents. Their broad blood ties united all together to create a social structure known in Lakota as 'tiyospaye' – wherein you became a member of an extended family. So whatever an individual did, such acts were measured by their overall effect on the tiyospaye. The foundation of Lakota life was affinity, which meant having a sense of belonging to one's community, living in harmony with others, a love of the earth, mutual trust and generosity, and above all, the love and value of children.

We in the 21st century like to think of these principles as commonplace and universal. As we have come to discover, they are not, but in my Sioux-obsessed childhood, I experienced them every day, and they stand me in good stead now in my old age.

Roy Bainton
Mansfield, September, 2010.

General George Crook, (1828-1890) U.S. Army, Department of the Platte:

'The buffalo is all gone, and an Indian can't catch enough jack rabbits to subsist himself and his family, and then, there aren't enough jack rabbits to catch. What are they to do?'

Quotes from Crook's staff:

'The Sioux are the finest light cavalry in the world.'
(Un-named officer).

'Foemen far more to be dreaded than any European cavalry.'
General Charles King.

'They were the best cavalry in the world; their like will never be seen again.'
Captain Anson Mills.

'Fine fighters, brave, great tacticians .... If I were an Indian, I often think, I would greatly prefer to cast my lot among those of my people adhered to the free open plains rather than submit to the confined limits of a reservation, there to be the recipient of the blessed benefits of civilization, with its vices thrown in....'
General George Armstrong Custer

FLYING HAWK ON CRAZY HORSE:

'I HAVE BEEN in nine battles with Crazy Horse; we won them all. Crazy Horse was quiet and not inclined to associate with others; he was in the front of every battle; he was the greatest leader of our tribe; he told me this story once:

'I was sitting on a hill or rise, and something touched me on the head; I felt for it and found it was a bit of grass. I took it to look at; there was a trail nearby and I followed it; it led to water; I went into the water; there the trail ended and I sat down in the water; I was nearly out of breath; I started to rise out of the water, and when I came out I was born by my mother. When I was born I could know and see and understand for a time, but afterwards went back to it as a baby; then I grew up naturally -- at the age of seven I began to learn, and when twelve began to fight enemies. That was the reason I always refused to wear any war-dress; only a bit of grass in the hair; that was why I always was successful in battles. The first fight was with the Shoshones; the Shoshones were chasing the Sioux; I, with my younger brother riding double; two of the Shoshones came for us; we started to meet them; I killed one of them, took his horse; we jumped on him, my brother and I double, and escaped.'

Interview with Flying Hawk, Sioux Warrior, in *Firewater and Forked Tongues* by M. I. McCreight, Trails End Publishing, Pasadena, CA 1947 p 138 – 139

My Uncle Charlie on his nephew's obsession:

'Let's face it, lad – you'll never be an Indian as long as you've got a hole in your arse...'

Crazy Horse and The Coalman

PART ONE:

AFTER THE BOMBS.

Crazy Horse and The Coalman

1. MEET THE HEYOKAH

*"It is a good day to fight! It is a good day to die!
Strong hearts, brave hearts to the front!
Weak hearts and cowards to the rear!"*

Crazy Horse, Little Big Horn, 25 June 1876

I always found the curmudgeonly words of another Hull resident, Philip Larkin, *'they fuck you up, your mum and dad'* puzzling. As with our social fabric in general, there are probably as many variations in parenthood as there are in any other familial relationships. Perhaps it's all rooted in that peculiar old shibboleth – class.

Contrary to Larkin's view, my parents didn't 'fuck me up'. My blood father, a convicted bigamist, inadvertently tried to, but that early wound was healed by my mother's lack of choice. She simply had to get on with life and start anew. Looking back down almost seven squally decades, despite the trauma of incessant poverty my parents went through, they gave me and my step brothers nothing but happy memories. As the maxim goes, 'a boy's best friend is his mother', and that was certainly true in my case. She died, aged 58, in 1973 following an operation for a strangulated umbilical hernia.

In retrospect, her fraught, shortened life, like that of my noble stepfather, seems positively Dickensian when compared to that of her children. Had my poor mother lived longer, what might I have been able to show her? What fulfilment of her modest dreams – a proper holiday, a trip to Europe, some comfort, could I have provided? At least Dad, with 20 years as a regular soldier, had seen the world. The furthest Mam got was London, and then only for a few days.

So as I write, I look at the photograph of those two burdened individuals, my parents, and wonder where they got the energy to smile at the camera and carry on. Their lives and responsibilities unfolded without a template or a brief. There were no 'parenthood' gurus in those days – not that we knew of. They staggered between each domestic challenge and hardship through a minefield of economic adversity. They were, in many ways, like us, their children; innocent, yet still possessing a dream, a sense of adventure. I loved them then, and although both long gone, I love them now, and this little book may be about me, but really, I am what they made me. As for the other friends and relatives featured, they were all good people in their own way, despite the way my memory may have represented some of them. I have changed the names of some deliberately, as I have no intention of causing offence. I have no doubt the majority of them are long dead, so the reader must accept that the views of them expressed here only represent my immature perception of them as a child. Age, like distance, lends enchantment, and with that thought in mind, I accept that memories of people and incidents can become exaggerated. Sixty years on, with the rigours of life stacked up behind me, it becomes obvious that the help the various people in this story gave to my immediate reckless family, probably with some reluctance, was, with hindsight, nothing short of pure kindness and compassion.

Sometimes, on summer mornings, the essence of childhood returns. Its visitation is fleeting, like an unseen postman bringing a postcard of memories. It has an odour of cut grass, a buzz of bees and a slight rustle of breeze-blown leaves. It has memories of waking up on white pillows and through the window, seeing that blackbird flit across the bright blue backdrop of a June sky. In the weeds at the end of the vegetable patch I once saw the ghost of my grandfather. No-one believed me. This day in this memory will see the spirits of General George Custer facing up to Tsunke Witco, a.k.a. Crazy Horse, not on the greasy grass by the Little Big Horn River, but on the velvet, green manicured expanse just beyond the tree line at the northern end of Willerby Golf Course (now known as Springhead Park Golf Club). It is complete with the exhilaration of trouble-free innocence, of days without worry, of red admiral butterflies and their white cabbage comrades, of daddy longlegs, frogs and tadpoles, our den in the deep, dark hawthorn hedge, and the tall tree where, should we dare to climb to its highest limb; legend had it that you could see distant London. It smells of Dad's Punch tobacco roll-ups, bonfires and the steam from Mam's copper boiling up the weekly wash. It has an insect soundtrack punctuated on long, sometimes morose summer afternoons by the drone of John Arlott's dense cricket commentaries, and a winter background of howling winds interrupted by the hobnailed boots and fortnightly rumble of the coal man as he tipped his hernia-inducing bags of life-giving fuel into our bunker.

Yet just a few yards away, through the bushes beyond our cabbage patch, the well-heeled, pipe-smoking golfers in their silly trousers always lost their balls.

What did those golfers know about Little Big Horn? Not as much as the eight year old sunburned boy with the sandy hair. This was the kid who had joined the Wold Road Library in 1950 where he pestered the assistant in the Adult section for anything she could find on the Sioux. Even his innocent friends at Wold Road Juniors had little idea of how they were frequently being manipulated in his regular war games on the golf course. One day his friend, Gilbert, who lived in a posh house which actually had a bathroom, asked why he *always* had to be George Armstrong Custer. The answer was that the scabby-kneed whippersnapper from Wymersley Road was *always* Crazy Horse; Barbara Addison was *always* the chief's first wife, Black Buffalo Woman, so it was natural that because Gilbert was posh, he would forever be Custer.

"But what about Custer's other battles," Gilbert would wail. "Can't I *ever* win?"

"Not against Crazy Horse – *never*…"

This memoir is in four parts. That's another Sioux thing. Why? From my standpoint, it covers four locations where I grew up; Hull, Halifax, Hornsea and back to Hull. From a Sioux standpoint, 4 is a sacred number to Native Americans. All events and actions are based on this number, because everything was created in fours.

- Four elements make up the Universe; earth, air, water and fire

- There are four things above the Earth; the sun, moon, sky and stars.

- There are four directions; North, South, East and West.

- There are four seasons; Winter, Spring, Summer and Autumn.

- There are four divisions of time; the day, night, moon and the year

- There are four parts in everything which grows from the ground, the roots, stem, leaves and the fruit.

- There are four kinds of things which breathe; those that crawl, those that fly; those that walk on four legs; and those that walk on two legs.

- Mankind has four fingers on each hand; two thumbs and two big toes together that make four.

- There are four periods of human life; birth, adolescence, manhood and death.

- Indian People speak of four virtues, a man should possess; bravery, generosity, wisdom and endurance.

- Men go by themselves for 4 days and 4 nights before an important ceremony. Indian ceremonies last for 4 days.

- Four days after death, a feast is prepared in ceremony.

Yet although the spectre of Crazy Horse would endure, the days of the battle of the greasy grass ended in 1952. There was another chapter of childhood about to open up.

Wet. Cold and wet. That's another way I remember parts of it. Cobbled stones, stone walls; beyond that a bleak, empty landscape. Our short-trousered legs were cold in those days. Crows and Magpies would look down on us from wet slate roofs and I imagined that they were feeling sorry for us. In their black shiny plumage and limitless sky they had everything they needed. Not like us. The tops of our wellington boots chafed our calves and our balaclavas made our necks itch. Our clothes, usually army surplus, were itchy, oversized and uncomfortable. I often wondered how Tsunke Witco kept warm in those South Dakota blizzards. But he had buffalo robes and a tipi with a central fire. He didn't need to go to school. He hunted and fished and listened to stories, then slept in his warm, smoky darkness, enjoying his visions as the razor-sharp wind outside piled up the drifting snow against the taut walls of his buffalo-hide home.

Going home across the drab moors in the jagged wind, it always seemed dark, always winter. When the clouds lifted and the stars broke through I would amble along, gazing upwards, whilst wondering what kind of a life stretched ahead for me. And when I would finally stumble into the remote, gloomy, damp house with its paraffin tilley lamps and the smell of methylated spirits and burning candles, the answer to my homeward pondering often seemed to be one bereft of hope. If our parents had only managed, by their advanced years, even after fighting a war, to achieve this stark level of existence, then what chance would I have? The people down the hill had gas, electricity and running water. Many of my classmates even had bathrooms. Why was the life we led so different from theirs?

Of course, as Oscar Wilde said, 'Who, being loved, is poor?' So, in that respect, we were rich. But in the candlelight on cold nights I couldn't see that truth.

But that period was only one chapter in many. There were others with dark streets, the forlorn, fogbound horns of anchored ships waiting in the muddy Humber by busy docks, terraced houses, backyard chicken coups, the smell of fish and outside toilets. Other episodes had their own bleakness, urban as well as rural. However, although there was always material poverty, we enjoyed a wealth of love. There was always social embarrassment, but this was eclipsed by defiant pride. We may have been part of the lumpen proletariat, yet like Crazy Horse, we were not always docile. We rebelled when it was required.

The beauty of childhood, however, is innocence. In the western world, unless one becomes incredibly rich, or is born to privilege, childhood is the only time in life where our day to day existence is someone else's responsibility. Our parents put the food on the table. They provide a bed and a roof. Our teachers educate us. All we have to do is … play. Some of us played more obsessively than others.

Maybe Tsunke Witco's life didn't have any similarities at all to that long-gone kid on the golf course, other than my immature desire to share his spirit. I've always struggled to synchronise any elements of my psyche with his, and I know how futile an effort it's been. In later life, the beacon of inspiration could well have been Leon Trotsky, Spartacus or El Cid, and even though Orson Welles remains such a breathtaking muse, all four of these icons combined produce only a glimmer of motivation alongside the stimulating incandescence of Crazy Horse. What connection to his culture could I possibly have? How could I have lived by his heroic ground rules? I couldn't really contemplate killing a man or even ride a horse, let alone one without a saddle. I hate confrontation. As a paranoid flyer, I almost fill my pants on a jet plane, and wouldn't go anywhere near a rollercoaster. Spiders scare the shit out of me. But when you're a kid, things are simpler. You don't realise how dangerous it is to climb a tree until you fall out of one. So what kind of a Sioux would I have been? A lad's life in the north of England seems so contrary to that of a free-living Lakota Sioux in the Black Hills. But all these years later, after reading more, I know where I would have fitted in, because I've figured it out.

A contrary clown, the *Heyokah* holds total wisdom and through laughter and opposites, teaches the People. He's a kind of sacred trickster, determined to make you question if what they actually do or say is correct. So, ultimately, those who come into contact with the Heyokah will listen, then puzzle, then attempt to figure it out for themselves. I'm not claiming the Heyokah's total wisdom, but one of their wise traits was that they always walked backwards, which is exactly what I'd be doing if a battle was imminent. The Sioux had a little song about the Heyokah:

Aho Heyokah!
Make me laugh so I'll be human again.
Allow me to see my crooked path
And the Trickster as my friend.

Aho Heyokah!
How contrary you can be,
Yet you make me learn.

Aho Heyokah!
The jokes on me,
But next time it's your turn!

The Lakota, like other nations, also had their homosexuals, known as *Winktes,* men who didn't want to fight, and, often wearing female clothes, worked on domestic chores with the women. They were tolerated, if not exactly encouraged, but apart from the sex angle, I think I'd probably be happy to share their tipi. So, were there any links at all, genetic or otherwise, between me and Crazy Horse? Perhaps not. Yet oddly enough, I was born at four in the afternoon in the fourth month of the year. Four has always been my lucky number. I started some of my best jobs in April. As we've seen, Lakota culture is based on the number four. Everything connects: I look at the Buddhist Wheel of Life and it has Four Noble Truths: life means suffering, the origin of suffering is attachment, the cessation of suffering is attainable, the path to the cessation of suffering. So we're all connected. The power of the world always works in circles. A man's life is a circle from childhood to childhood, and thus it is in everything where the power moves.

The centre of the universe is everywhere; Pine Ridge, Little Big Horn – Halifax and Hull.

2. NO TIME FOR HITLER

*'What is the matter that you don't speak to me? ...
I'd be better satisfied if you would talk to me once in a while.
Why don't you look at me and smile at me? I am the same man.
I have the same feet, legs and hands, and the sun looks down
upon me a complete man. I want you to look and smile at me.'*

**Goyathlay (Geronimo) to
General George Crook, US Army.**

In the summer of 1866, the great Sioux War Chief Red Cloud made his position clear with regard to the influx of white men into his sacred territory. At a special council he told the gathering;
"The white man lies and steals. My lodges were many, but now they are few. The white man wants everything. The white man must fight, and the Indian will die where his fathers died."

It's a sobering thought, but by grandfather was about six years old when Red Cloud called his meeting. He was born in Bielefeld, Germany, and sadly died two years before I became Crazy Horse. He left us in 1947 when I was just four years old. He'd left Germany as a young man and worked as a ship's cook on the route between Liverpool and New York. The misty myth in our family has it that whilst living briefly in America, he married a Native American girl whilst working as a manservant to Frank Winfield Woolworth, founder of the now defunct High Street stores. Damn right I want to believe it, although I realise it's probably untrue. This is because I can't see the sense of abandoning a potential career in New York City for the life of a railway clerk in Sculcoates, Hull. How the hell did Granddad end up in Hull after such an American existence? It would be like swapping a life in St. Tropez for one in Middlesborough. But if it was true – and when I was a mewling kid it always *was* true – then I imagined

I had some extremely tenuous connection to the free men of the Black Hills, the Great Plains, or the forest, Monument Valley – wherever Hollywood suggested the Indians lived. Yes; it was so genetically obvious - that was why I went red in the sun and not brown like my little mates. I was a Sioux warrior, and I would accept no other identity. And Granddad, as Aryan as they came, had his truck with the white man, too. The breed in question were the whiter than white variety – the Nazis, whose ascendance had changed his mind about returning to Germany in 1932.

He'd been a railwayman, a cook, a baker, a manservant. He was tough, square, angular, and blue-eyed with a shock of white hair which had once been Nordic blond. He liked listening to Beethoven and Brahms on the radio, kept chickens in the back yard at Queen's Terrace off Portland Street in Hull, just a stone's throw from the bus station. People liked old Karl - at least before the war came along. For a while he had a small baker's shop in Convent Lane. Even then, before I was born, he was very old and sometimes absent minded, yet people loved his bread and they spoke well of him. Even when Mrs. Clutterbuck returned a loaf one day, its fluffy white interior displaying the bizarre grin of the old man's lower set from his false teeth, he exclaimed "*Mein Gott*! I have been looking for those since yesterday!" Yet the exchanged banter was humorous and good natured, sweetened by a new, denture-free replacement loaf and some cream buns. That was, until the war. In the first war, they had locked him up with his fellow 'Enemies of The King' in a camp on the Isle of Man. This time, with the Luftwaffe ascendant, it was different. The man who once sold bread to his talkative neighbours had bricks thrown through his window, and we were not admitted to the air-raid shelter. We'd become the nasty Krauts, the 'enemy within', a situation Granddad, still measuring out his flour and yeast, found quite puzzling. His dough was British, but it was kneaded with German hands. Yet his three sons were risking their lives for England in the Atlantic Convoys and the ranks of the British Army.

"*Vy? Vy* are they so crazy?" He would ask; "I am the same man!" Such is the fear and incomprehensible effect of war.

But for me, the brief Granddad days were days of joy.

When the sun shone on those immediate, peaceful post-war mornings I would awake to the smell of freshly baked bread, and on the landing outside my bedroom would carefully avoid looking at the smirking Laughing Cavalier who stared sinisterly down from the frame on the wall at the top of the stairs. The lure of fresh bread nullified the fear engendered by the Cavalier's follow-you-everywhere eyes.

Downstairs in the kitchen, in front of the cast iron Yorkist range where the fire flickered, Granddad would serve me a hot muffin oozing with melting butter. The daily baking of bread was – even in his 80s - the heartbeat of his life. It began at 6.30 am every day; first rising of the dough, a concentrated kneading followed by a second rising at 7.30, then into the oven by 8.15. Sometimes he would mutter along in German as he worked, others he would hum some ancient, indecipherable Teutonic song.

The war was a huge tragedy for my Mam and Granddad. In the mid 1930s she had met a German sailor, Rudolf. A merchant navy engineer, apparently he was the consummate Bremen gentleman, and by all accounts good looking to boot. Mam's brothers, my uncles Laurie and Frank, however, both well-travelled sailors, knew what was going on in the Reich, and had a strong inkling of what was coming. When he docked in Hull, Mam would invite Rudolf to visit, where he had the added bonus of being able to converse in his native tongue at will with Granddad. However, if Laurie and Frank were ashore at the same time, things became frosty. This was a pity, because Rudolf had serious reservations about the Nazis. He said he preferred being away at sea to get away from all the 'Heil Hitler' stuff back home. Yet Laurie and Frank were having none of this. Laurie knew how many ordinary Germans had been sucked into Hitler's charismatic honey trap, and as his sister Freda's big brother, he felt he had a certain responsibility.

"There'll be a war," he would say, "and where would you be then – a collaborator! There's thousands of good Englishmen out there and you choose a German!"

This attitude always puzzled Mam, especially with our German ancestry. Yet in later years she understood Laurie and Frank's attitude. As the prospect of war loomed they had both attempted to join the Royal Navy, yet were turned down. Laurie always maintained that it was something to do with the family surname, Kohler. This had produced a bitterness which was overcome by a burning desire to prove their absolutely British credentials, a mission they would complete with honour during the inevitable conflict.

The things Rudolf told Granddad about Hitler and his goose-stepping empire made the old man laugh. He'd already seen it with Mussolini's pompous fascism, and he considered everything about the Third Reich to be nothing more than an end-of-the-pier music hall show. He was very sad when he realised he was wrong, but not as heartbroken as Mam was when Rudolf was called into the U-Boat service. After the spring of 1939 she never saw him again.

When the war eventually ground to a bloody halt, Granddad laughed out loud when he heard that Hitler was dead. There was no time for *der fuhrer* in our house.

"Ach! I *said* it would happen! That *dumkopf*! I knew he would ruin Deutschland and he has *done it*! Now I can *never* go back!"

Meanwhile, in 1942, Freda, my Mam, had married a British soldier; an act of honour which she hoped would impress her fighting brothers. Sadly, as time would tell, honour was a characteristic missing from my father's arcane, albeit British character.

In the long, pre-school afternoons I would watch the clouds scudding by over the broken, bombed and toothless landscape of Hull as Beethoven's Ninth Symphony – or one of the other eight – boomed out through our chipped Bakelite radio as Granddad hummed along to the main themes. Mam would dust and sweep and polish, take the rag rugs out into the yard, hang them on the line and beat them with a carpet beater. After an hour, they would be brought back in and, like a playful puppy smelling his first horse manure, I would roll on those rugs absorbing the freshness of the air in which they'd hung. Then I would watch Granddad feed the chickens, and wonder about his long life and all the things which had happened in the world since he left Germany as a young man. If only I had been older, and known which questions to ask. But it was too late, I suppose.

My biological father, originally a miner from Barnsley, was still in the Army, serving as a Private in the Lincolnshire Regiment. I'm not sure what wartime battles he fought in, but I do know that one of his duties was guarding what was left of the pier at Withernsea. Presumably Rock Bob's novelty confectionery emporium must have been a major target for the Panzer Divisions. Anyway, I didn't see much of him. In fact, I can't recall seeing him at all until I was probably about three and a half, and the occasion was a catastrophe which would shape our lives for years to come. The storm broke one sunny afternoon in Queen's Terrace.

I had been across for a treat at the house of Mrs. Moses, an aged neighbour whose name suited her seemingly Methuselah years. She was, looking back, an obvious survivor from Victoria's reign. The only sound behind the delicate lace curtains of her pristine dwelling was the dull, rhythmic 'clunk' of her grandfather clock, and when it struck loudly on the hour I always jumped out of my tiny skin. It was the kind of house where Edgar Allan Poe would have spent his time with his ear clamped to the wall, listening for the agonised, coffin-bound scratching of a premature burial. Yet for a curious toddler, with its potpourri fragrances of faint carbolic, mint, molasses and surgical spirit, it was weirdly irresistible.

Her tall, mahogany sideboard supported an array of glass domes, beneath which were a stuffed cat and two long-dead paragons of the taxidermist's trade, the motionless parrots

Captain Billy and Mr. Pedro. Often she would talk to these rigid, silent corpses as if they were still about to flutter into some kind of cackling vocal life. In fact, not fully understanding death, I sometimes put my ear to their glass coffins and expected a response. But Mrs. Moses was a kind old lady with a hobby most boys could admire; she made her own sweets. She had all those characteristics you'd expect for a lady of her Victorian vintage; a hair-sprouty wart on her chin the size of a nipple, *pince nez* spectacles, lace shawls, and as she passed close there was a distinct aroma of lavender. Pride of place in her confectioner's art was her cough candy. It nestled on a lace doyley in a nickel-silver bowl, all chunky, brown, sugar-dusted translucent rough cubes of it, piled up like the abandoned masonry of an Assyrian tomb, a delight to crunch in tiny trainee teeth despite its tongue-splitting menthol after burn. She had a glass case with shelves in her kitchen and I would ask her to read to me the mysterious labels on the jars there, because they had funny names; something called 'squills', 'tincture of tolu' 'ipecac' and 'oil of gualtheria'. No doubt had Mrs. Moses, in the company of her black cat, Alastair, lived a couple of centuries earlier, she would have spent every Friday on a ducking stool on the banks of the Humber. But that product of her geriatric alchemy, cough candy, was something else. It never seemed to cure coughs, but it beat the hell out of my Junior Liquorice Smoker's kits, complete with sweet cigarettes and coconut tobacco.

On that hot afternoon I had made it back across the terrace to our house with my mouth stuffed with cough candy and enough of the rugged delicacy stuffed into my pockets to provide ballast for a trawler. Once inside, with Granddad snoozing in his chair, I was accosted by Mam who barked "Open your mouth!" No doubt the viscous brown gunge I displayed looked like something from a sewer, although my breath did undoubtedly have all the fragrance of a recently disinfected orthopaedic ward. She was about to tell me to spit it all out and chastise me for once again pestering Mrs. Moses when she suddenly stopped and looked into the middle distance, listening. I heard it, too; the steady marching rhythm of hobnail boots clattering down the terrace. My father was in the back yard, feeding the chickens, when there was a loud knock on our front door. Mam wiped her hands on her apron and went to open it, and I stared down the passage to see two stocky, tall military men wearing red caps. I couldn't hear the conversation clearly, but they were both invited in and, as was the custom with visitors, installed in the front room. Granddad snoozed on, I stood in the middle of the kitchen still digesting my candy, as Mam cruised past, called Father from the yard, after which they both disappeared into the front room. I beat a hasty retreat upstairs, carefully averting my eyes from the omnipresent Laughing Cavalier, and hid my surplus cough candy in the old biscuit tin under my bed, where it clattered into place between several platoons of lead soldiers.

When I came back downstairs, I was puzzled to see the two red caps escorting my father, complete with his army kitbag, from the house. It would be over twenty years before I would see him again. Although he had often referred to me as his 'precious little lad', it transpired that he was a bigamist, already married before the war to a lady in Barnsley, where he already had several other precious little lads and lasses he had conveniently forgotten about. Going up to bed that night, leaving my mother in the kitchen in floods of tears, I finally faced up to the Laughing Cavalier. You don't scare me, I thought. Grin all you like. Even though I couldn't quite understand it, I'd just experienced a shaft of reality. Even today, every time I see his enigmatic face, I sneer back at him. Piss off, go and frighten somebody else.

Hitler had taken one of our families – my Mam's younger brother, Stanley, who, although he'd survived D-Day, had been shot dead by the SS in the Falaise Pocket in Normandy in August 1944. But now, in our house, down our little terrace which had stubbornly dodged the Luftwaffe's bombs, the war seemed as if it was far from over.

Crazy Horse and The Coalman

3. THE TRIBE

*'We do not interfere with you, yet again you say,
Why do you not become civilised?
We do not want your civilisation!
We would live as our fathers did,
and their fathers before them.'*

Tsunke Witco / Crazy Horse.

Perhaps the difference between us and the Sioux was that we lived on the reservation right from the start. As I remember it, both socially and physically, that reservation was in quite a mess. The U.S. Cavalry may have had devastating field artillery, but they didn't have an air force like the Luftwaffe. Hitler was, according to my Uncle Charlie, a Hull docker of some renown, who we shall meet eventually, 'a nasty little bastard who bombed my pub.' I'm not sure which pub it was, (probably The Sportsman on Hedon Road) because we didn't see Charlie too often, but we had regular exchange visits with his wife, my Auntie Millie. But Charlie was right. Herman Goering really had it in for us. I've since wondered about those German pilots and bomb-aimers. How could they be so cruel to this family – with a German granddad, for Christ's sake, down there in an innocent fishing port? Because of them, post-war Hull was in a sorry state. Yet that fractured and destroyed urban landscape was great for a four year old. Unlike today's media-driven climate of paedophilic fear, back then the idea that a gang of four or five year old urchins held little significance. As long as we came home when we were expected to, the world beyond the front door was ours. I would go out with my slightly older mates on hot, dusty afternoons and crawl through bombed-out houses and explore rubble-filled craters with absolute glee. At around five o'clock,

I needed to be back within earshot of my Mam, who would call me in for tea. In those days it was usually a doorstep sandwich of Granddad's bread smeared with brown Tiger Sauce or, if we were lucky, pork dripping with all the pungent brown jelly bets left in.

Here's where the Sioux and I part company for a while, because the affinity between various strands of our extended family was threadbare, to say the least. Although some bonds of affection in our immediate lineage existed, there was only as much *tiyospaye* around with us to accommodate three tipis at the most. But we were still a tribe, no doubt about that. In the streets around us lived various members, uncles, cousins and aunts and there were others dotted around further from the city centre. Following my poor Mam's shock at having my bigamist father carted off by the Military Police, there was an initial wave of sympathy. It also helped that she shared the house with Granddad. With my dad out of the picture and complicated, divorce proceedings under way, Mam had to get a part time job. She became an assistant cook at a the Regal restaurant, which was on the top floor of the cinema building of the same name on Ferensway, close to the bus station and the Paragon railway station. In those austere times, I recall her coming home and telling us bizarre stories about food preparation for the consumption of the remnants of Hull's middle class. Rancid steak, well beyond its use-by date, would be hammered into tenderness on the chopping board and sprinkled with vinegar to disguise its taste of decay. Choice cuts of cod, rarely in short supply in what was then Britain's premier fishing port was dyed pink with cochineal and served up as salmon. It made us all glad that we were poor, rather than posh snobs, because at least we knew what we were eating. Mam's part time work meant that at certain times of the day, because she thought it unfair that Granddad should bear total responsibility for me, I would be farmed out to my Auntie Bertha in Spring Street.

Bertha was kind and good hearted, often cheerful, but the

matriarch from hell in many ways. She was a total stranger to the concept of hygiene. Forget Mumbai's slum dog millionaires. Alexander Fleming could have scraped Bertha's front doorstep with a teaspoon and come up with enough Penicillin to keep Harry Lime happy for months. My earliest memories of being cared for at Bertha's were the peculiar smell. It was a slightly nauseating, sweet-tinged odour which seemed at its strongest in the entrance passage just by the front room door. It was no good going to Bertha's in the morning, because she preferred to stay in bed until around mid-day. This prolonged act of relaxation was to accommodate her literary bent, as she worked her way through a cartload of historical romantic paperback novels each week. Therefore, propped up in bed after a good night's kip was the perfect place to catch up on the dastardly deeds of rugged Captain Posternblast as he sullied the honour of the innocent heiress Miranda Moleskin. So, like some reluctant sacrificial goat, I would usually be pushed through the door at around 1 pm, by which time the portly Bertha would be holding court by the parlour fireplace. She was habitually still in her frayed dressing gown, from which protruded her ample bare legs, fleshy trunks turned into reddened approximations or Ordnance Survey maps as the heat from three shovels of crackling No. 3 Engine Coal, courtesy of LNER, swelled her veins into a lattice-work of B roads.

The hygiene aspect of Bertha's domain began at this point. The parlour table was covered with a frayed, stained oil cloth which displayed the tacky consistency of a trawler skipper's oilskins. On this stood a forest of pint milk bottles, their vintage signified by the varying shades of green, congealed gunge they contained, usually around an inch at the bottom of each bottle. The idea of rinsing out milk bottles and placing them on the doorstep was an alien concept, so every so often a few would be removed and tossed into an old tea chest in the back yard. Naturally, at my tender age, none of this seemed as bizarre as it does now. I simply imagined that Bertha had plans to start her own dairy one day; she certainly had bottles

enough to accommodate the product of a healthy herd of Friesians. In later years I realised that Bertha was Miss Haversham minus the tragedy, although she'd collected many more gastronomic relics than an ancient abandoned wedding cake. Yet I was lucky to be the recipient of her kindness, and like most kindly matriarchs, her first concern with children was ensuring we were fed. Despite the time she spent in her horizontal literature studies, she still managed to turn out a cooked dinner for her husband when he arrived home from work, although the unhygienic provenance of such feasts left much to be desired. I witnessed an example of this one day when I asked if I could use the toilet. "You know where it is," she said, "out in the yard – but if you're having a number twos, I need to know."
I told her I simply wanted a pee.
"In that case, be careful with your aim..."
When I lifted the sneck on the lavvy door and peered inside I realised what she meant. Parked on the wide, round and stained wooden seat were four pot basins; one contained custard, two blancmanges, and the fourth a strawberry jelly. I pointed my miniscule manhood as carefully as possible and managed not to add any unwanted condiment to these delicacies. Back in the house, she informed me;
"You didn't pee on our puddings, did you?" I shook my head.
"Good – they'll be set nicely for when your Uncle gets home."
It also takes little to turn a toddler off the idea of green vegetables, but I remember one Sunday venturing into her yard where, under the outside tap stood a galvanised bucket full of Brussels sprouts. My 8 year old cousin appeared, tried the toilet door and was greeted by a manly grunt from within which signified adult occupation. Undaunted, the lad pulled out his willie and sprinkled freely into the bucket of sprouts. I've had a bad thing about sprouts ever since.

Lunch (or dinner time, as we knew it) for me and Bertha's

kids was a culinary revelation in itself. The first experience of this is vivid. I stood by the festering table-top arboretum as Bertha looked me up and down like a farmer assessing the value of a prize pig. Then she leaned forward, scratched her burgundy-tinged calves and said

"Cheer up, son! Are you 'ungry?"

I mumbled in the affirmative. She pointed to the sideboard. Scattered around on this were additional ripe milk bottles, quite a few half-open packs of margarine and the remains of several abandoned bread loaves, ranging in size and epoch from expired, crumbling bricks of jade mould to one at the very end which seemed almost fresh and 90% intact. Bertha clapped her hands.

"Aye, that's the one! See if y'can find some fresh marge as well."

I found some margarine which was as yellow as possible and not in a state of semi-liquidation and presented her with this and the bread loaf. She bent down to the hearth and picked up a sturdy bread knife. She stood the margarine on the arm of her chair, then to my abject horror hoisted up the hem of her dressing gown and grubby nightdress high enough to be accused of indecency, revealing two wide, flabby thighs, their livid complexion in stark contrast to the toasted rouge roadmaps of her lower legs. I experienced a new wave of revulsion as she took the bread loaf and clamped it high up in this dank, cellulite valley, its crusty top nestling somewhere I dreaded to think of. She took the breadknife, delved into the margarine and began to butter the end of the upright loaf. Then, clasping the breadknife she proceeded to horizontally cut a slice from the loaf, which, once detached, she aimed at me with all the nonchalance of someone chucking a Frisbee on a beach. I caught it in both hands, my thumbs plunging through the thick margarine.

"Go on then," she snapped, "get it eaten up!"

Here's another way the Sioux Indians and us differed. Crazy

Horse and his warriors bathed regularly in the river, often several times a day. The Sioux were a clean people. I would later look back in sadness at the fact that some members of my tribe differed radically in this respect. For example, even in my own home the tin bath only came into the kitchen on Sunday nights, and depending upon who'd enjoyed the grey, scummy water before you, when it came to your turn for immersion in this lukewarm epidermal stew of congealing bubbles and biological detritus the notion of ending up 'clean' was highly challenged. I much preferred the daily hand, face and neck washes in a bowl on the kitchen table.

My visiting period at Auntie Bertha's house lasted only a few weeks, and was brought to an abrupt end by Mam. When she came to collect me when returning from work each day, she would always comment on the way home about the foul pong in Bertha's front passage. (The one in her house, anyway). Mam used to let herself in at Bertha's house and one warm afternoon she arrived a little early and did something very daring. She pushed open the front room door. Inside were the remains of a three piece suite which looked like the decomposing cadavers of three hitherto unknown animals.

In the corner of the room, standing on four house bricks, was a deep, galvanised metal bath, covered with an old pine door. Mam stood in the room and grimaced. This was definitely where the foul odour was coming from. She bent down and smelled the back of the dead sofa. She shook her head. Then she went over to the old tin bath. She lifted the paint-peeling door and the gush of foulness which filled the room had me retching.

Clinging to the underside of the old door was a thick white furry substance streaked with black. It came away in chunks to reveal a dense green slime at the top of the bath from which jutted the remains of what appeared to be rotting fabric. It transpired later, after quite an unpleasant family rift, wherein Mam was accused, with some justification, none the less, of 'interfering' that several months before Bertha had decided to put some stained bed sheets and dirty towels, plus one of her husband's mucky old boiler suits into soak, prior to an eventual wash day. Sadly, Captain Posternblast and his literary retinue had intervened too many times and erased his biggest fan's memory of the covered bath and its forgotten contents. Mam said later it was a lesson in science. I later came to think of it as a similar process to the way they make Soy sauce, Tofu and other bean curds, although I doubt if they use boiler suits and bed sheets.

Another interesting member of the tribe was Uncle Dan. I do not know what his relationship was, but he was some kind of con man who lived by the seat of his pants. Well, 'con man' is probably a bit severe, come to think of it. He was more like those characters one reads about in the Wild West who sell snake oil and elixirs of life, then move on to the next state before the Sheriff or Marshal catches up with them. Dan always had some door-to-door scam going. One of his favourites was *'Doctor Dan's Amazing Foot Reliever'*. This involved Dan in placing an order with a local printer for a few hundred small square manila envelopes, printed with the title of his remedy and the following instructions;
1. Take a bowl big enough to accommodate your feet.
2. Remove stockings or socks. Men, roll up trousers.
3. Bring just over half a gallon of water almost to boiling point.
4. Pour water into bowl and let it stand for a few minutes.
5. Empty the contents of this packet into the water and stir until dissolved.
6. Carefully check that the water is not too hot, then immerse your naked feet in the bowl and soak for 30 minutes.

So, what was the formula for this efficacious universal relief for the worn-out feet of the working class? Answer: Colman's Mustard Powder – just a dessert spoonful. The odd thing was – it worked. At nine pence (that's 9d in old money) a packet, he needed only to sell to 26 households to pocket a pound. And Dan had the staying power and the energy to work street after street in Hull, so that by lunch on his first day he had usually covered his printing and mustard costs, and he got repeat orders. Mam even knew it was plain old yellow mustard powder but she often had a soak because she believed Dan and knew that mustard had some anti-inflammatory properties. As to his *'Doctor Dan's Smoker's Linctus'*, this glutinous mix of lemon, glycerine, liquorice and eucalyptus was more expensive to produce because of the formula, and especially the bottles, many of which Dan bought from round the back of a bent chemist's shop on Holderness Road. Yet many people liked this palliative, despite the fact that in some cases, if taken to excess, it could produce a rapid case of involuntary, trouser-filling diarrhoea. With his little brown attaché case and his pin stripe demob suit Dan, tall, Brylcreemed and gangly, was a well known character that, in another age and with the right education, could have made a million. Unfortunately, he had a weakness – Craven Park dog track. Whatever Dan made, it went to the dogs. On the days he did win, he'd get drunk and buy a round. On the more numerous days he lost, he simply needed to inflict more diarrhoea on a community suffering with aching feet. He was, to coin a phrase, mustard.

Then there was my kindly Uncle David, whose job was so romantic it outstripped Spitfire pilots and deep sea divers. David was a train driver. He was a benign man with a soft spot for me, because on the odd Saturday when he wasn't manipulating an LNER 4-6-2 Pacific locomotive and several hundred passengers in the direction of Edinburgh, he would call for me and take me down Hull's busy Whitefriargate, just for fun. It meant an iced bun and lemonade in Lyons Café, and a choice of toy, up to 2/6d in Woolworths. Happily married though he was, he did often express despair at his hapless spouse's culinary prowess. I remember one day listening to him complain to Mam.

"I came in – been on the Newcastle run – at work 12 hours,

and she'd made a pot of tea. When I poured a cup out I found she'd forgotten to put the tea in. So it was just hot water. Then I asked her what was for dinner. She said 'peas on toast'. Yes, half a tin of Bachelor's peas on a dry crust. Good job I'd had a Cornish pasty at Darlington…" I've no idea what happened to poor Uncle David, but for years I treasured the little metal Lancaster bomber he'd bought me in Woolies. It would have been a 4-6-2 locomotive but they didn't do those for half a crown.

The Uncle who left them all standing for entertainment value was, however, Uncle Charlie. I always likened him to Crazy Horse's mentor and senior strategist, Chief Red Cloud. Red Cloud was older than his warriors; an outspoken man of great wisdom he was in his late 40s in December 1866 when he gave Crazy Horse his first notable glory, when the fiery young warrior was chosen to lead a decoy party to trap soldiers from the newly constructed Fort Phil Kearney, built in contravention of the US government's treaty with the Sioux, along the Bozeman Trail. It was a tragic Christmas for the garrison. A stupid and arrogant young Captain, William Fetterman, who had done well in the Civil War, held the same opinion of the Plains Indians as most of his contemporaries. He thought they were unskilled savages, no match for the organised militarism of the white man. After rashly claiming he'd personally scalp Red Cloud and bragging "With eighty men I could ride through the whole Sioux nation," he was given his chance. His eighty men may have 'ridden through' the Sioux but they didn't emerge at the other end – all were killed. Of course, I had re-enacted the so-called 'Fetterman Massacre' (known to the Sioux as the battle of Piney Ridge) in a field close to Willerby's golf course. The Gypsies often camped there in horse-drawn caravans, and as a reward for their kids showing me where to look for mushrooms, (thereby scoring me extra Brownie points with Mam) I let them be members of my Sioux war party. Looking back, they were probably as near to a

British version of the Lakota than any other kids we met – and they even had horses! My much put-upon classmate, Gilbert, already weary with his recurring role as General Custer, was forced to play the doomed Fetterman.

My own Red Cloud, Uncle Charlie, was a member of the crème de la crème of Hull's huge proletariat. He was a docker. He was also a very popular worker with the picky, awkward and often corrupt stevedore managers and their foremen on the docks. In those days the so-called 'casual' scheme of dockland employment was in full swing. It had all the nasty capitalist flavour so well described by Robert Tressell in his masterpiece *The Ragged Trousered Philantrophists*. This meant that, when there were fewer ships in dock, there was always a much larger pool of labour than was required on a particular day, and the stevedore's hiring area became something resembling a 19th century farm labourer's hiring fair. If you knew the man doing the hiring well enough, and could afford it, you might be able to surreptitiously slip him a pound or two the night before a big ship was due to unload. Perhaps fifty to a hundred men would gather, and, based purely on favours, bungs, association or nepotism, perhaps half would be hired that day, with the remainder sent home on no pay.

The Hull dockers were a breed apart. If I considered myself as a Sioux, then the dockers were definitely the Apaches, in which case Charlie should have been Geronimo, but I wasn't all that interested in the Apaches. Sure enough, Hull's dockers, like their counterparts in Liverpool or London, were militant and big-hearted. But the Hull lads seemed to have their own sense of humour, and their own brand of sartorial inelegance, a long way from Savile Row. You could often tell a docker by his old gabardine mac, its belt often replaced with string, his greasy flat cap and what seemed to be standard-issue wellingtons, turned down at the top. Most dockers rode bicycles and in the early morning and late afternoon Hedon Road would be clogged with a whirring, gruntingly breathless mass of Sturmey Archer gears moving along in a steady slipstream of tobacco smoke. The Hedon Road dockers, those who worked mainly on King George Dock, had an off-site tribal meeting place opposite the junction for Marfleet Avenue.

Today, the Klondyke Café would inspire nothing less than shock and cardiac arrest among our zealous Health and Safety Executives and even more so for the Jobsworths of a Council's planning department. The Klondyke is hard to describe, and the following does suffer from some embroidery, but let's imagine that in the early part of the 20th century several ornate Victorian Hull salons and cafes (and possibly brothels) were demolished for one reason or another. The interior wall panels, all oak and rosewood arches and marquetry, would have been salvaged by some astute local domestic scrap dealer who may have thought that some nouveau-riche trawler skipper or fish merchant might fancy them for his Citizen Kane-type San Simeon semi-detached castle in Kirkella. Wrong. Someone with a working passion for frying pans, kettles and teapots snapped up all these ill-matched wooden walls at a bargain price and nailed them together in a ramshackle, interconnecting structure. This was topped with a wrinkled felt roof, its multi-angled broken-toothed skyline reminiscent of the random peaks of the Swiss Alps. To give the whole thing a vague sense of uniformity, that same someone, a welcome, would-be caterer to the dockland welly-boot workforce, had bought a job lot of cheap, dark purple paint and slapped it on.

Well, that's as I remember it, but lest you think my flippant description denigrates the Klondyke, let me assure you that it was a fine institution, run by good people who knew their customers – what they liked, what they could afford. You got value for money at the Klondyke; somewhere cosy to sit for a brew and a smoke, and all just minutes away from the docks. Where did the name come from? Who knows – but looking at the place one could indeed imagine hordes of muddy forty-niners and panhandlers dining there between gold strikes. The rambling edifice was interrupted with a few small windows added here and there, and once the cooking ranges and tea urns had been installed, the good ship Klondyke was in business. I don't know when it was built, but it survived well into the 1970s. Today it's a patch of scrappy wasteland by a huge roundabout, but in the 1950s this was the hub of dockland intrigue and nefarious planning, all accompanied by copious amounts of sweet tea in pint pots, bacon banjos, fried egg sarnies, assorted sponge puddings and custard, with not a burger or hot dog in sight. Uncle Charlie was wise enough to have spent a great percentage of his working life in the cosy, nicotine-hued micro climate of the Klondyke.

Charlie was a labouring aristocrat, a bill-hook artisan, a philosopher and supreme raconteur. He spent fewer days at home than many, and not particularly because of bribery. As he said to my Mam "I *know* things. I keep my eyes and ears open. I could bust those buggers down on the docks wide open with what I know – and I could name names, give times and dates. And they *know* it... the bloody lot of 'em!"

Coming home from school and finding this crafty, astute, funny and wise rake holding court in our kitchen was a sheer delight. The odd thing was, though, is that although we often had visits from his wife, Auntie Millie, we never had a regular joint visit from them as a couple. It was always one or the other. Millie used to speak in hushed tones of abject horror to my Mam about Charlie's comings and goings. She often referred to him with a shudder, using a strange, arcane term;

"Ooooh! He's a bugger up the back!" And my Mam would sit there gravely 'tu-tutting' with each new whispered revelation.

But for a young lad, having Charlie himself in the house was a dream. First of all, like most uncles, he'd often press half a crown into your hand and give you a sly wink. But it was his stories of a character that purportedly lived with him and Millie – his Mother in Law. I never met the woman nor did I know her name, and I've never had her existence proven, but

Charlie always referred to this domestic mystery monster as 'The Old Vinegar Bottle'.

Sitting by our fire with a mug of tea and wreathed in blue smoke from his roll-up, he would lean in towards me in a conspiratorial way and begin yet another convoluted epic which would feature the docks but always culminate in a starring role for The Old Vinegar Bottle, all frequently punctuated by my wide-eyed queries.

"Now then – I had a hard day on the dock yesterday. I was tired. We were unloading bananas from South America and something terrible happened."

"Was it something frightening and scary?"

"Oooh ... *not half*! I'd better not tell you. You'll have nightmares."

"Oh, go on, Uncle Charlie. I'll not be scared – *honest!*"

"Well, I warned you. We were down in number two hold and the hook came down from the derrick and I fastened on a great big crate of bananas. But the lid was loose."

"How big was the crate?"

"Nearly as big as this room. But when I looked closely at the dark crack where the lid was being pushed open, there was something moving. It was something long and spiky, and covered in bristles."

"A hairy snake?"

"Don't be daft – you never see hairy snakes – they get shaved every morning. But then there was another long bristly thing and it was twitching, so I took the hook off the strop and got my mate Harry Sugden to pass me a crowbar and we took the lid off altogether. Then we saw it. It was ... *oooh! Horrible!*"

"What was it?"

"First one leg came out, then another, then another and another and another, then another three, all spindly, spiky and twitchy and hairy, and I jumped back and Harry coughed in his trousers and nearly fainted."

"But – but *what was* it!?"

"What's got eight twitchy hairy legs?"
"Was it a South American dog?"
"A dog with *eight legs*? Blimey – I'd bet on that at Craven Park! No, something much scarier than a dog. Something creepy and crawly."
"How big was it?"
"As big as you."
"But … but what *was* it?"
"A spider!"
"As big as *me*? Really – that big?"
"Too true, old son. An Argentinean goat-eater."
"Oooh – Uncle Charlie – but spiders eat flies…"
"Well, not this one. If he ate flies he'd need buckets full. He was looking for goats. He was yellow and black and hairy and had all these shiny little black eyes and whiskery jaws like hacksaw blades, and he chased Harry all over the hold, and poor Harry was coughing in his trousers – and worse."
"How can you cough in your trousers?"
"He was trumping. It's summat blokes do when they're really, really frightened. And I think he pooed himself as well."
"*Uuggh*! But spiders can't be as big as me … can they?"
"The South American ones are. I heard they had one as big as a garden shed."
"What happened? Did you kill it?"
"No. It got its hairy legs on the rope up to the derrick, scuttled up, leg over leg, like a sailor up a Jacob's ladder, ran across the deck, scaring everybody, then jumped overboard onto the dock and ran away."
"Oh … *no* … have they caught it yet?"
"No. It's still looking for goats."
"But there's no goats around here …"
"Well, not any longer there isn't. It was hungry. But it's being looked after. It'll not starve."
"Is it in a zoo?"

"No. It's round the back of the Klondyke. It likes sweet tea and meat pies. Somebody from Chipperfield's Circus is going to take it away."

This exotic horror story was destined to haunt my dreams for years. Every time I saw a bunch of bananas I would imagine a hairy leg protruding from the tropical yellow mass. Even the thought of such a beast having touched a banana was enough to put me off the fruit. When Charlie told his tale, I didn't have the courage to persist with further questions. After all, I felt sure he'd tell me that the beast might have followed him to our house and was already tapping at Mrs. Moses's door with some cough candy in mind. So, discretion being the best part of valour, I changed the subject.

"What happened when you got home?"

"I was tired out, especially after seeing that spider. It was dark, and when I got to our front door, who do you think was waiting for me?"

"Auntie Millie?"

"Naw... she was in bed, reading a book about highwaymen and naughty women who take men upstairs in pubs. Naw... it was the Old Vinegar Bottle. She was standing there with a lighted candle in a jam jar in one hand, and a bucket of hot soapy water in the other. You know how she always has a job for me to do, don't you?"

"Yes. But why are you scared of her? She's only an old lady, isn't she?"

"Only an old lady? The *Old Vinegar Bottle*? Ha! A *lady*? Oh, no. She's a wicked old witch."

"What – is she ... like ... *magic*?"

"Oh, aye. She mixes potions in the kitchen. She calls them Irish stew, porridge or Semolina Pudding, but I know what her game is. She wants to cast spells on me to make me her slave. And it works. Last week I had to do all her ironing. Great big cotton knickers and nighties you could hold a circus in, and a brassiere big enough for a couple of footballs. I was up all night."

"Why did she have a bucket of soapy water?"

"Well, here's what happened. I was standing there in the dark with my bike, and she held the candle near my face, and I was looking at the hairy warts on her chin and her broken nose, when she said "Put yer bike away, lazy bugger, and then roll your trousers up and scrub the front step." So I did. There was a scrubbing brush and a cloth in the bucket and I scrubbed the front step, then she made me scrub the floor in the hallway, and all the time she was stood there in her furry slippers made from dead cats and her big flappy apron with swastikas on it with her arms folded, laughing at me. Your Auntie Millie never interferes, because she knows full well that with the Old Vinegar Bottle around, she can have an easy time. So being on the docks, you see, even with big hairy spiders, is easier than going home."

Decades later, long after Charlie had been hoisted by God's golden derrick into that heavenly afterlife dockland, I was once talking to my Mam in front of a roaring fire about 'the old days'. It was near Christmas, 1972, not realising that within a few weeks she would be dead at the age of 58. The subject of Uncle Charlie came up, and between the laughter I heard her sigh once more,

"Aye, he was a bugger up the back..." Of course, I was then an adult with my own family, and I'd had seven years at sea, so despite the very open and adult relationship I had with Mam I ought to have known better when I decided to ask her

"I always wondered – is that a particularly Hull saying?"

"What is?" she asked.

"*'He's a bugger up the back...'*".

Mam leaned forward and poked the fire, chuckling.

"Oh, you know when your poor Auntie Millie used to talk to me all in whispers and looking worried?"

I nodded. "Yes – so...?"

"Well, *that* was what it was all about. Charlie was a bugger."

"A ... *bugger*?" Mam looked incredulous and shook her head.

"Oh, come on, son, you're a man of the world. Do I have to spell it out for you? He liked to stick his thing up her bottom."

❖ ❖ ❖ ❖

Crazy Horse and The Coalman

4. NUTTY SLACK

*The Great Spirit gave you two ears
and only one mouth,
so you can talk half as much as you listen.*

Cheyenne Saying

The coal man was a major figure in our lives before the advent of central heating. No doubt to some people he still is.

In the days before that corporate wind of death we've come to know as privatisation, the coal man was one of many well-known characters in a well-knit community, one of those people who visited our homes regularly for one reason or another. Others, like the rag and bone man, arguably a descendant of the bloke who used to wander around during the Plague singing 'Bring out your dead!' usually walked the streets pushing a hernia-inducing handcart with one hand whilst blowing a bugle or ringing a bell with the other. I don't recall ever giving him any bones – they were our dog's province. I suppose they used to make glue from such organic donations. Yet I often presented him with a pile of old socks, Mam's old drawers and Dad's tattered underpants in exchange for a balloon or a goldfish. The good thing about the vanished rag and bone man is that he left us with a nice, terse addition to our vocabulary of Hull insults, to whit;

"You need the thick end of a ragman's trumpet!"

We'll get around to the importance of the coal man eventually, but it's worth examining other members of this pageant of forgotten characters. There was a street vendor dispensing hot mushy peas, usually consumed with plenty of vinegar. Whereas garden peas, small, delicate, fresh and sweet, remain the premier culinary garnish, the bullet-hard marrowfat pea is the commando of the legume army, soaked overnight and then boiled with a dash of bicarbonate close to death to form that morass of semi-solid green, calorific fuel. Mushy peas are to flatulence what petroleum is to a flame-thrower, producing a distinct aroma which adds little to your popularity on the top deck of a bus. Another peculiar personage, not exclusive to Hull, was the street corner news vendor. There were several in Hull, all flogging the *Hull Daily Mail* between mid-day to about 6 pm. Perhaps there were odd pockets of intelligence, but in the main, if there was some urban central casting department which specialised in characters representing contaminated toxic tramps with learning difficulties crossed with Quasimodo, then it offered full employment. It was amazing to discover how many loudly vocalised variations there could be of the simple cries "Hull Daily Mail!" and the more semantically challenging "Hull Daily Mail – First Edition/Sports Edition!" These usually came out at maximum decibels as

"Hooderry mer!" or "Yerulldermayall!" as well as "Hoddimeyer - vestishun!" or "Hoomeyer Spots!"

Usually found lurking around Paragon Station was a character even Dickens would have found difficult to dream up. Often in the company of his sidekick, the bizarre Eva, Roland was a colourful kind of Troll who passengers had to face before emerging into the city. He was a long-haired wiry man of indeterminate age, probably early 50s, wearing an open overcoat, a spotted red bandana around his neck, and a kind of adapted spiv's trilby, complete with a feather, the brim of which was turned up at either side to produce a distinct Sherwood Forest look. He was a riot of strange utterances and random whistles, and his mental 'otherness' allowed him to get away with acts of petty sexual harassment which would, today, have you clapped in a cell in ten minutes. These usually involved the deft use of his knobbly, polished walking stick, which he poked under the hems of the skirts of passing lady pedestrians, lifting them to provide a quick flash of stocking top, accompanied by one of Roland's odd whistles. Still at the lower end of the chain were a series of irregular oddballs who would knock on the door and greet the lady of the house with the query "D'yer want 'yer drains doin', Missus?"

This insalubrious service could be had for anything from sixpence to half a crown. It involved the unsavoury eccentric getting down on his knees, rolling up his sleeve past the elbow, and after removing the grille from said drain, plunging his naked hand and arm down through two feet of stygian gunge. Any blockages found would be hauled out in a black, gelatinous lump; dead rats, clumps of dog-ends, wads of rotting leaves and human hair. The odd thing about these drain men was their strange animal passion for their job. It was an ugly activity and the appearance of its devotees often matched its repugnance. Bad teeth, wheezing breath, the odour of which might fell an Ox, unkempt hair, greasy old jackets. I often stood by and listened to their grunts of primeval satisfaction as they discovered something lumpy, and the extraction of their slimy limb from the foul hole would be accompanied by a grotesque sucking sound. The drain man was a close relative, I think, of the knife sharpener. Sometimes, the knife sharpener would combine drain de-clogging with his premier craft, but Mam was never keen on having a man whose unwashed digits had groped in biological Hell handling our kitchen utensils. The knife sharpener was often welcome, with his bicycle specially adapted with an extra chain to drive his stone sharpening wheel. Of course, we also had those eternal door step pests, the Jehovah's Witnesses, but sometimes Mam used to tell them we were Jewish. In fact, for a while I thought we might well be Jewish, which, as I approached the age when Bar-Mitzvahs occur, worried me, but thanks to my Dad's Catholicism, parts of my anatomy have remained intact. I've usually followed Mam's inspired method of disinformation with an opening gambit to the Witnesses (and their close relations, the Mormons) of declaring myself a Buddhist who believes that Jesus was a Venusian.

Occasionally, probably at least once a year, the chimney sweep would come around. In general appearance and demeanour he was a close cousin to the coal man.

Then there were the real street heroes; the dustmen. Today they've become the hapless, un-co-operative and underpaid drones of the privatised 'where there's muck there's brass' garbage moguls, and are now designated as 'Environmental Waste Operatives'. In the distant days before Mammon squatted on the pot of civic pride, the dustmen were a cheery and welcome band of weekly callers in ex-army leather tabards who would manfully hoist a galvanised dustbin onto muscular shoulders and complain not a jot that it contained the still smouldering embers of a week's coal fire ashes, guaranteed to leave a scorch mark on their vests. These whistling, singing junk humpers would take anything away, and their willingness to do so always resulted in a generous tip from most families at Christmas. Sadly, the only tip they'd get from me today would be "Don't tie your shoe-laces in a revolving doorway".

Still with us, although a dying breed, are the milkman and the postman. Like the great economic mainstay of the Sioux, the buffalo, both of these animals are approaching the point of extinction. It seems hard to believe now, but even in the 1960s in Hull, if one posted a letter before 9 am in the morning, there was a good chance of it being delivered the same day elsewhere in the city in the second post before 1 pm. The morning post almost always arrived before 9 am, and you knew who your postman was. He had his round from the day he was employed until retirement. Today, probably under the appellation 'Printed Material Delivery Operatives' you'll be lucky to get your post before 2 pm, with a different postie doing the round every week. As for the milkman, like the postal service, he's surely doomed. Few potential employees these days could muster the self-discipline required to climb out of bed at 3.30 am to cruise endless streets on a slow electric milk float loaded with freezing dairy products. After all, they might miss Breakfast TV. No, once again, the supermarket has sealed off that social avenue. We always knew our milk man. Oddly enough, I know mine today, he's called Andy, who's done the ever increasing round for nigh-on 40 years, yet when he retires next year, we're laying bets that his tinkling float will become the dairy equivalent of the *Mary Celeste*, an abandoned rusting ghost in a shut-down bottling plant. In some areas of Hull, we even had a lemonade man. He'd collect your empties and leave you with a fresh supply of Dandelion and Burdock and Sarsaparilla. His appearance was sporadic, but for us kids eagerly anticipated.

There was a penultimate personality on the roster of house callers who will have his own chapter later on. In come parts of Britain he was known as the Tally Man. We knew him as the Club Cheque man. From my infancy right through to my teens, we had the same club man. His name was Ken, or, as the family preferred to call him 'Uncle' Ken. Club cheque men were the predecessors of Visa and MasterCard. For all intents and purposes, they were really *Cosa Nostra* loan sharks minus the baseball bat and knuckle dusters. They usually intensified their visits just before the start of each school term, when families needed money for school clothing. The epic of Uncle Ken and his association with our family ultimately drove me into joining the Communist Party, so we'll cross that bridge when we come to it.

Finally, the hardest grafter of them all – the coal man. The milk man brought us sustenance and vitamins. The postman provided news, good and bad. The dustman took our rubbish away. But the coal man kept us warm, whilst at the same time being the most expensive visitor of all. I never quite figured out why, but in our family, paying the coal man was always a difficulty. Dad would come home on Thursday nights and put his brown manila pay packet on the table, yet once the cash had been divvied up, the coal money always seemed a pound or two short. If you lived in a densely populated area, you could work a system where you dealt with two or even three coal merchants, but once the balancing act of paying a few shillings here and a few shillings there broke down, unless you paid up all the debt then you could end up with no coal at all, and that meant complete domestic misery.

The Sioux kept warm in their tipis burning a mixture of buffalo dung and wood whilst wrapped in thick buffalo hides. There was plenty of horse shit around in Hull, but we never tried burning it, and buffalo droppings were even harder to some by.

In Portland Street in the late 1940s we had a coal man called Manny Ogden. It was always difficult to assess the age of coal men, because after delivering to half a dozen houses, they all looked like members of the Black & White Minstrel show, and wouldn't have looked amiss warbling 'Mammy' as they heaved their sacks into your coal house or bunker. Manny Ogden (his first name was, apparently, Manuel – Mam said it was because his mother had been to bed with a Spanish sailor) was Schwarzenegger huge, and contrary to his supposed flamenco heritage, possessed a shock of blonde hair poking out from his fossilized, encrusted ebony cap, with ice blue eyes, a fact which made him look more like a camouflaged member of the SS *Liebstandarte Adolf Hitler* on a night mission behind Russian lines. He could clatter to and from the horse and cart in his hobnailed boots with such rapidity, disgorging three bags of anthracite into your bunker in the time it took to pour him a cup of tea. Mam had heard naughty rumours about Manny. There were at least three women she knew in the Portland Street area who had, apparently, offered him their physical favours in return for his nutty slack. Of course, nutty slack isn't the best thing for domestic fireplaces; it's dusty and cloggy, and burns slow, so the ladies only went so far (apparently above the waist) for a supply. But for two bags of top grade house coal, a pork dripping sandwich and a bucket of water for his horse, Manny got the full drawn curtains and locked front door treatment. How he balanced his employer's books was his problem, but venturing out to work in winter's coldest days must have filled the virile Senor Ogden with an element of sweet anticipation. Manny was the first of many coalmen we would know, and, bless 'em all, those we owed more than we could pay still delivered, even though we'd lock

the doors, draw the curtains and hide in breathless silence.

Occasionally, probably at least once a year, the chimney sweep would come around. In general appearance and demeanour they were the close, sooty-faced Jolson cousins of the coal men. I often wondered what a chimney sweep's house might be like. Sure, it would have a clean flue, but no doubt there'd be soot on the chairs, in the beds – everywhere. These are just some of the characters I remember. I know there were others.

Before my own family left Hull and temporarily went west in 1954, there were three stages to my existence. There was my birthplace, Queen's Terrace in Portland Street, then the glorious hut by the golf course, and a brief sojourn in a brand new Hull City Council house on Bilton Grange shortly after the Coronation in 1953.

As the gloomy post war days began to fade, Queen's Terrace seemed to gather a depressing, sombre ambiance. Although it had seen us through the war years, and was the place of my birth, it was also the exit point for my biological father's part in my life. His departure and trial, followed by imprisonment, took its toll on my Mam, and Granddad was beginning to slow down and suffer sporadic bouts of illness. I recall him sitting in the kitchen one night talking to Mam, and pleading;

"The boy needs a father. You can't bring him up alone. You need to have a man in the house. I will not be here much longer." This caused me to think that perhaps he'd changed his mind and was indeed going back to Germany after all. I would soon realise the truth. Eventually, some of Mam's friends set her up with a blind date, and one spring night there was a knock on the front door. Mam asked me to go and answer it. Standing before me, nay, *towering* over me, was six and a half foot of square-jawed ruggedness in a pin striped demob suit. I was just about the height of his hands, and they fascinated me. They were huge, with rough, long fingers.

They could have strangled an alligator, no problem. I was further fascinated by something exotic; peeping out from the neat cuff of his blue shirt, on his wrist was a snake's head tattoo. Who the hell is *this*, I thought – a pirate? He leaned down towards me like a dockland crane and smiled, his blue eyes flashing.

"You must be Roy, then?" I nodded nervously and mumbled a stuttered confirmation. His voice was a deep, rich tenor.

"Well, Roy, tell your Mam Stan's here."

We were to see a lot of Stan over the next few weeks. From snatches of conversation I put his story together. Stanley Bainton was a regular soldier, a sergeant, no less, with 20 years' service under his belt with the East Yorkshire Regiment, much of it spent in places with funny names such as Rawalpindi. He was an orphan whose childhood made Oliver Twist's experiences seem like the life of Little Lord Fauntleroy. At the age of eleven he was employed in the streets of Bridlington, selling fish from a handcart. The army then became his saviour. He was a good soldier, mentioned in despatches, brave, promoted, wounded and be-medalled. He'd fought in India, the Far East and Europe. He had been discharged from the Army with honours after a motorcycle accident in occupied Germany, and was now working as a carpenter and joiner. He proved his skills in that department by making me various ingenious wooden toys; a fully working crane and a wooden locomotive. As a potential Dad he was everything a boy needed. I had a sneaking suspicion that between the three of them, Mam, Granddad and Stan, that they'd decided upon this master of the chisel and spokeshave as my new father, and by the Autumn, it happened. I was kitted out in a very itchy blue sailor's suit for a wedding. Try as I may, I can't remember the details of what must have been a special and poignant day for Mam, but it was marred by

Auntie Bertha. As the happy couple left the registrars, some people threw confetti. Bertha, who seemed to think there was something suspicious about Mam's failed marriage to my father, Norman, shouted "It ought to be bricks!" Mam never forgave her.

Shortly after the happy event, Granddad didn't go back to Deutschland, but died peacefully in his sleep, happy in the knowledge that his grandson had a dad. I can't recall the actual funeral, but I do remember going into the front room where Granddad lay in his coffin on two trestles. He looked peaceful, as if in a deep sleep, and I wondered what his true, long life had really meant. His fine, square features, that shock of white hair. What was his past? Who were his family in Germany? What had he seen and experienced in America, and in those years on board ships at sea. He remains to this day a warm, mysterious memory. We never knew for sure how old he truly was. Some said 90, others suggested even over 100, but he was a good man. Thankfully, another good man had taken his place. His death didn't seem tragic to me in any way – he was enjoying a well-earned rest. His death was simply a natural and expected happening, and he had been instrumental in getting me a new father.

Naturally, I was pleased about it all. He was a big man, my new dad, and as tough as they came. I remember one event which placed him even higher in my estimation. We had an old Collie dog called Rex. One night, after we'd finished our tea, I was fooling around with Mam in a playful way, and pretending to be a boxer, moved towards her in what Rex assumed to be a threatening manner. To everyone's horror, the dog snarled and leapt upon me, sinking his teeth into my upper right arm and tearing a nasty wound, about three inches long, which immediately gushed blood all over the place. Stan grabbed the hapless Rex by his neck, threw him across the room and picked me up bodily. Cradling me in his arms, still in his shirt sleeves, my blood soaking into his shirt sleeves, he ran with me all the way to the Victoria Children's Hospital, where he sat with me, telling me stories of gunshot wounds in the war whilst a surgeon patched me up. For a few minutes I thought I was part of the Regiment, and then I fainted. The next day, Rex was nowhere to be seen. He'd been taken away and destroyed, and although I totally appreciated everything Dad had done for me, I knew that all poor old Rex had been doing was protecting Mam.

Dad had been working temporarily for Clover Dairies as a milk man. He hated the job, and every afternoon when he came home there was a distinct smell of cheese in the house.

But things were looking up. He'd resigned, and with his carpentry skills was finding plenty of construction work as the flattened city of Hull began to be re-built. There was also something very mysterious happening. Mam's stomach was expanding to the point where I thought she'd swallowed a football. I knew we all ate reasonably well, plenty of bread and jam, the occasional steak and kidney pie, fish and chips on Fridays, and we always had eggs, but examining my own insignificant stomach and comparing it to Mam's one day resulted in me asking what was going on.

Then one day a letter arrived. The Council had decided that our terrace, surrounded as it was by extreme bomb damage, was to be demolished. It said that we would eventually be allocated a new council house, but they weren't built yet, so that in the meantime we would be temporarily housed in an ex-military complex of Nissen huts on a place called Wymersley Road.

I was about to discover my new identity – Crazy Horse.

❖ ❖ ❖ ❖

PART 2:

Little Big Horn

Crazy Horse and The Coalman

5: COUNTING COUP

'Grown men can learn from very little children
for the hearts of little children are pure.
Therefore, the Great Spirit may show to them
many things which older people miss.'

Black Elk, Sioux Holy Man.

To win prestige in battle, the Plains Indians 'counted coup'. They performed acts of bravery in the face of the enemy, which were noted and recorded, and retold as fireside stories, a kind of precursor to the Discovery Channel. Striking your enemy with the hand or with a coup stick counted as a coup. The most prestigious act was actually touching an enemy warrior, then escaping unharmed; a similar activity (but with purpose and honour) to today's nasty teenage activity, (un)happy slapping. There had to be risk involved – death or injury, and stealing from your enemies counted. After each certified coup you carved another notch in your coup stick, or added another feather to your warrior headdress, which would signify your act of bravery.

By the end of my second year at Wymersley Road, my coup stick was so notched it was in danger of disintegrating.

Before leaving Queen's Terrace, there were people to say goodbye to. I had some good friends, Trevor and Colin. We were all equally poor. Trevor's father had been killed in Normandy, and his mother worked behind the underwear counter in Thornton Varley's, a department store. Poor Trevor was never very well dressed. In fact, few of us were. The seat of his pants was always hanging out and the notion of a handkerchief had by-passed his household, so that the cuffs of his shirts and jacket always bore a crystalline patina of congealed snot. Like all of us, the holes in his shoes were frequently repaired by having cardboard stuffed inside. That was fine until it rained. But come September it seemed to be the tradition that some wellingtons turned up, and these usually lasted as the sole footwear until the spring. Colin had an unfortunate affliction which Trevor and I, in our infant insensitivity, found highly amusing. He stuttered a lot. Conversations with Colin took three times longer than with anyone else. Once, when we were playing at being commandos on a bomb site at the end of Colonial Street, we'd reluctantly let Colin have the role of sergeant for the afternoon. As we planned our attack on our imaginary Germans, Trevor waved his 'sten gun', a bent piece of lead piping, at Colin.

"What do we do now, Sarge?"

"L – l – look out f-f-f-for the ber-b-ber-b ..." Colin's 'b's' went on for a while.

"The *what*?" enquired Trevor, impatiently.

"The ber-b-b-b-" I decided we'd simply have to lose to the Wermacht this time just to get out of this linguistic cul-de-sac.

"Argh! I've been *shot!*" I cried, "And *you've* been shot, Trev!"

"Have I? Oh, *right..*" said Trevor, who then clutched his shoulder and fell backwards. Colin stood up and yelled

"The b-b-bullets!"

Trevor was a year older than me and showed me how to make my first catapult. Colin was good at making bows and arrows with sticks and bamboo canes, something which would soon come in handy for a potential Sioux. We would spend our afternoons in target practice, knocking tin cans off the top of the perimeter wall which enclosed a strange and mysterious place called Corporation Fields. All we knew about this place is that it had once been a big vegetable market. With wartime it took on the character of the sinisterly secretive Area 51 at Groom Lake in Nevada. It had an impenetrable wall of concrete around it, but there were gaps which we could look through, and one of the things we saw was the fuselage of an aeroplane. There were also some odd noises – a kind of a high pitched whine, early in the morning and at night. Mam told us that as well as once being a vegetable market, it was also the place where they boiled crabs. Apparently, (although I never proved this) they were still bringing live crabs there and boiling them in huge coppers even after the war. Mam said the noise was the crabs 'screaming' in pain. The very thought of it made me shudder, although it never put me off a helping of fresh crab claws which Mam would sometimes bring home on a Friday afternoon.

Another person to say goodbye to was local hero Willie Rushbrook. Willie was probably in his 50s, and ran one of those local shops on Portland Street where you could buy just about anything. He had it all; bread, margarine, tinned goods, mops, buckets, meat pie and peas. The latter were Rushbrook favourites. Every day he'd bake up a batch of meat and potato pies in the kitchen at the back of the shop, alongside a bubbling cauldron of mushy peas and a two gallon pan of rich brown gravy. For 9d (that's probably about 8p in 'new' money) you could take a plate to Willie's and he'd dish you up a portion of pie, a dollop of peas and crown it with a dollop of gravy. The trick was running home fast enough without spilling it before it got cold. I seem to remember Willie as a vague shadow of Groucho Marx, with his horn rimmed glasses, dark moustache and always a trilby hat. His concession to health and safety was a pristine white coat, which made him look slightly scientific. And nothing went to waste in the Rushbrook kitchen. Many days my Mam would send me round to his shop with a large basin, which he's fill with cold mushy peas for sixpence. Yes, it was sad to leave Willie behind us.

I must have been just over seven years old when I first set eyes on our new home. At Queen's Terrace, despite a back yard with a small chicken run, the idea of a garden was sheer

luxury. There were a couple of post-apocalypse, crippled trees on the bomb site at the end of Colonial street, but that was the only greenery we had. The day Mam said "We're going on a trip to see our new house – it's out in the country" I initially wondered which 'country' she was referring to. France? Sweden? And so, all scrubbed up and wearing our patched best, we first walked into town to the housing department at
the Guild Hall to collect the keys. Then to the bus station. I knew straight away that wherever we were going, it must be beyond the city limits. Hull Corporation's blue and white buses and trolley buses covered all the inner city, but the routes of the dark blue and cream buses of East Yorkshire Motor Services fanned out at length into the great and mysterious unknown regions of East Yorkshire. So when we got onto an EYMS bus which displayed the destination 'Wold Road', I immediately had to ask Dad "What's a 'Wold'?"

"It means countryside where there used to be chalk hills. At the other side of the river Humber there's the Lincolnshire Wolds, and we're going to live near the Yorkshire Wolds."

The idea of 'chalk hills' was intriguing, but I never saw any. The lower deck of the bus was non-smoking, so we travelled on the upper deck, right at the front, so that Dad could enjoy his roll-ups. To me, the view was spectacular, as if I was in a low-flying plane. As the bus moved further and further away from the crumbling, war-blighted inner city, we began passing long rows of pristine semi-detached houses. Many had privet hedges, gates, front gardens and neat fences. Obviously, the Luftwaffe hadn't been anywhere near here. Maybe this was where the Germans had planned to live if they'd won the war.

At the very end of our journey, the horizon opened up as one of fields, trees and hedgerows. We left the bus, walked a few paces and turned left into Wymersley Road, and facing us was the old army camp, about a dozen low black buildings which reminded me of small aircraft hangars, each with a brick kitchen extension at the end.

The sky was blue, it was a warm, spring day and I could hear a strange sound, something I missed back in Portland Street. Birds were singing. If birds did anything in Queen's Terrace, they coughed. There was something wonderful about this place.

A lot of the open areas between the huts were overgrown with long grass, but as it waved gently in the breeze even this was exciting. Around the perimeter of this vacated military estate tall green trees grew, and apart from the soothing birdsong and the mild rustle of the grass, everything else represented peace, but it was a rural peace bristling with hidden potential for a young boy. What discoveries could I make here? What expeditions could be had, what adventures? The Nissen hut was certainly going to be a fascinating place to live. I asked my mighty new stepfather, always a mine of military information, why they called it a 'Nissen' hut. Naturally, he knew all kinds of stuff. He even knew the original guy's full name.

"Ah-a! He was Major Peter Norman Nissen of the 29th Company Royal Engineers. He'd been an engineer and a miner and in 1916 he constructed three prototype semi-cylindrical huts. The Nissen hut was first produced during the Great War – at least 100,000 were built. Nissen was awarded the Distinguished Service Order. Is that good enough for you?"

"Er.. yes. Thanks."

Even before Dad turned the key in the black-painted door I was energized, because I could see, running the whole length of the structure at the rear was an overgrown garden, running twenty feet to a dense barrier of hawthorn. Through the odd narrow gaps in this hedge, I could see tantalising swathes of manicured green grass. What was it? A park? A cemetery? Maybe it was a zoo – there might be elephants and monkeys in there. I was itching to find out.

Inside the new house, the first impression was one of space. I liked the idea, too, of everything being on one level. I looked at the kitchen, with its brick construction housing a huge, coal-fired washing copper, scrubbed wooden draining boards and massive pot sink. Of course, there was no bathroom, but there was a real luxury – an inside toilet! No more freezing, rain-lashed trips in your slippers for a wee or a poo in the back yard! The main living area was about twelve feet square with just one window and in the corner a cast iron fire place with a small tiled hearth. There was no flat ceiling, just the interior curvature of the roof, spanned by three wooden beamed trusses. There were three bedrooms; one, a kind of corridor, directly accessed from the living room, another off this, which I felt instinctively, would be mine, because it had a window facing that mysterious hedge, and a large 'master' bedroom at the end of the house.

The day of moving in, its fine details, have evaporated from my memory. All I remember is the joy of two summers living there. I can't recall any nostalgic pangs of leaving Queen's Terrace behind, and I know Mam was more than pleased to be going far away from that tight little enclave where she'd experienced the triple traumas of war, bigamy, and her father's passing.

At Queen's Terrace I'd been a pupil at my first school, Wawne Street Infants off Spring Bank. It was the kind of heavily disinfected mausoleum Dickens could have written a whole book about. If you arrived three minutes late (as I frequently did) the teachers, who, in retrospect seem to have been trained by Heinrich Himmler, (after all, one of the mottoes of the SS was 'sympathy is weakness') would indulge in their favourite daily pastime, ritual humiliation. Populated as it was by nervous kids from five to seven years old, its Dettol-flavoured scrubbed floors often succumbed to a stronger odour – hot pee. In addition, the ancient Edwardian patina of sweat and panic accrued on the all-in-one desks-cum-benches was often shot through with another early cherub-produced corrosive as many of us, overcome by state-induced terror, managed to shit our ragged pants. This had one advantage – it always got you sent home for the day, although the crab-like walk, pursued by flies, was never comfortable.

But the trials of Wawne Street were behind me. Once we'd moved into our new home at Wymersley Road, I'd had time to explore the area. It was terrific. We were on the extremities of Hull, with open countryside to the east and north, and I had discovered what the greenery was beyond the hawthorn hedge, which straddled a 4 foot deep dry ditch. It was a huge expanse of velvet green, pitted here and there with sandy bunkers. It was the first golf course I, and my Mam, had ever seen. Each day I would peer out through the hedge at the strange, exotic creatures ambling from bunker to bunker. Unlike my Dad, or Uncles, these were not 'ordinary' men at all. They were like portly visitors from some florid planet where the law stated everyone had to dress in a very silly way. Funny tartan hats with red pom-poms; plus-four trousers (crudely referred to once by visiting Uncle Charlie as 'shit catchers'), tucked into multi-coloured socks. Black and white shoes, which reminded me of clowns. And what a lazy bunch they seemed; their odd, long leather bags, some with little wheels, bristling with golf clubs, were carried by someone else, a kind of servant, who Dad referred to as a 'caddy', which until then I thought was something you kept tea in. And then there were the daft little white balls, and the almost infantile efforts to get them into a tiny hole with a flag in it. What on earth was all this about – and something which required a couple of smooth, green undulating square miles, too, where you had to be some kind of member to even walk on the grass? Yet despite its innate stupidity, golf fascinated me. I had a slight interest in football, but only because it had a touch of battle about it, with studded boots and shin pads. But golf? I began to think that one day, when our end of the course was clear, I might try it out for myself and see what it was all about.

In September 1950, I was taken to my new school, Wold Road Juniors. This was in a totally different league to Wawne Street.

We had desks accommodating two pupils, rather than the long, multi-occupied Oliver Twist type workhouse efforts I was used to. There were big windows looking out onto a splendid playing field, and the teachers actually seemed pleasant. I also found it rather exciting to share my desk unit with a pleasant girl called Barbara Addison.

I had just started receiving my weekly edition of a fine comic called *The Eagle*. When I took a copy to school and showed it to my delicious little desk-mate, she asked me an odd question.
"It's not a girl's comic. It's got all sorts of boy's heroes. Which one do you like the best?"
There was no argument. I hadn't really got to grips yet with Crazy Horse.
"Dan Dare, Pilot of The Future."
"Oh. So do you want to be a spaceman when you grow up?"
I thought about it. Perhaps I did, however, I wanted to impress her. I took a risk.
"Yes. I think I'd like to be on a rocket to the moon."
She glanced at *The Eagle* for a moment then looked at me rather seriously.
"Can you ride a bike?"
A bike? I had an old three-wheeler which Uncle Charlie had rescued from the dustmen. Maybe that would do.
"A three wheeler?"
She shook her head and let out a cynical little laugh.
"Oh, Roy! You are funny. How can you steer a rocket ship if you can't ride a two-wheel bike? I bet Dan Dare can ride a bike."

It was a disappointing truth, because she was right. I had once tried to ride Dad's bike but I kept falling off, because my feet wouldn't reach the pedals. Sure enough, outer space did fascinate me intensely, but if I wanted to impress Barbara Addison I'd better shut up about it.

Not far from Wold Road School stood the local library. Although I was to maths and arithmetic what Billy Bunter would have been to hang gliding, I had learned to read pretty well and this meant much more than simply comics. I also wrote a lot, and Mam encouraged me by buying me cheap exercise books and pencils on the rare occasions we went into town on a shopping trip. So one day, upon leaving school at 4 pm, I stopped off at this wonderful library and asked for an application form to join. I was disappointed that I would only have access to the junior library section, but it was a start.
The next day, with the form signed by my parents, I got my ticket. Just holding it in my hand was exhilarating. All those books – all stacked on shelves, waiting for me to devour them.
On my first browse I found a few illustrated books about cowboys and Indians but I began wonder why it was always the cowboys winning in every skirmish. Some of the books which had colour pictures of the Plains Indians particularly inspired me. The colourful outfits; the war bonnets, the buckskins. I managed to find a book about Buffalo Bill and when I took it home Dad said that at one time Buffalo Bill, and his Sioux Indians, had come to Hull. Something resonated in me; to think, I was standing on the same soil that Sitting Bull had once stood on. Indians – in Hull, no less! Mam also took me to see a film starring Henry Fonda called *Fort Apache*. I found some if it hard to understand, but the crazy hapless character, an officer played by Fonda called Owen Thursday, who causes so much trouble with his military incompetence, seemed a long way from the soldier types I'd been reading about. I couldn't stop talking about the film, and one night, as I played with my box of lead soldiers Dad listened to me going on about Owen Thursday, and said

"That's what General Custer was like. He was an idiot. Daft as a brush." Until then, I hadn't made up my mind about Custer. He was always portrayed as a hero, as in Errol Flynn's *They Died With Their Boots On*. But my Dad's attitude, him being a military man with an interest in these things, drove me further into the Indian camp.

I still consumed eagerly the adventures of Dan Dare in the *Eagle* every Thursday, yet the Indians were dominating my life. After I'd read everything I could in the library's reference section about the Sioux in particular, I was still left with the worry that in many ways they weren't getting a good press. They were always 'savages'.

Not long after my 8th birthday I plucked up courage to speak with the nice lady behind the library counter.

"Are there any proper books about red Indians?"

"What do you mean – all our books are 'proper'."

I found it difficult to express myself.

"Well – did any of the *real* men – the cavalry and the cowboys – not made-up ones like in comics – did any of them write books about the Indians?"

"Well," she said, smiling, "I think they did, but I think they'd be hard reading for a little lad. And they're adult books for grown-ups. But I'll see what I can do."

I can't recall that kind woman's name, but a few weeks later when I was wandering around the shelves she called me over.

"I've got something from a library in Leeds. If you look after it, and bring it back on time, you can borrow it on your ticket."

My heart throbbed in anticipation. The title, on a slightly worn light brown leatherette cover, said it all.

Our Wild Indians - Thirty-Three Years' Personal Experience Among the Red Men of the Great West.

It was by somebody who had a name like an American cowboy town – Dodge. Every spare minute I had during the next two weeks was spent with my head in this book. Much of it, probably written in a late 19th century style (it was published in 1890) was, to my junior brain, incomprehensible, as were the various military terms and ranks. But when he wrote about the Indians, he seemed to have plenty of respect. Richard Irving Dodge was a Lieutenant Colonel with the infantry based in the Black Hills. He appeared to have some admiration for the Cheyenne, saying that they were a great and dignified fighting force. This was more like it.

My friendly librarian found me other books of a similar nature, and an uncle who had immigrated to Canada sent me a book published in America. *Crazy Horse; the Invincible Chief* was written by a man in Los Angeles called E. A. Brininstool, also known as the 'Cowboy Poet'. Here was someone who knew the Sioux for what they were – fearless and noble warriors, fighters for freedom. What I gleaned from this detailed account of Crazy Horse's life and sad death confirmed my deeper suspicion – Custer was a big-head and an idiot and Crazy Horse was a hero.

In fact, he was more of a hero than Dan Dare, Pilot of The Future, because Tsunke Witco was a real man who had actually lived. I had a new hero. I couldn't desert Dan Dare, but Crazy Horse began to tower over everyone else, and as I told Barbara Addison – I bet *he* couldn't ride a bike, either.

My fascination with the golf course and its weird and wonderful occupants continued. I had soon made a circle of friends at school and they would come around to our house where we began making a splendid den in the dry ditch on the golf course's edge. This den was totally enclosed by the dense hawthorn bushes, and we would sit down there in a semi-circle reading our comics. The most intelligent of my friends, Gilbert, was a bit posh. He lived on Wold Road in a house with not only a bathroom, but – a telephone. I was intrigued by his taste in comics. He read the *Wizard*, sometimes the *Rover*, but always, without fail, the *Hotspur*. Not for him the highly entertaining *Beano* adventures of Biffo the Bear, Hairpin Huggins, Happy Hutton, Skinny Lizzie and Gertie the Goat (and after 1951 – best of all, Dennis the Menace). Not for posh Gilbert the *Dandy's* Desperate Dan, Korky the Kat or Keyhole Kate. No; Gilbert was a *Wizard* and *Hotspur* boy. The United Kingdom in that immediate post-war decade may have been battered and thrashed by five years of war, and yes, we'd lost

India and the Empire was rapidly slipping away, but dammit, chaps – we were still *British!* Nowhere was this fact more evident than in Gilbert's comics. For example, the *Wizard's* star performers were a couple of characters called Skipper Sam and Spadger, a pair of crafty colonials who appeared to run an offshore African enclave called Spadger's Island. This imperial outpost was, apart from the white faces of our heroes, populated entirely by ... brace yourself ... *'niggers'* who all spoke something like this *"We ham diggin' de coal mine but we am savin' de coal dust fo' de face powdah fo' de nigga ladies!"* (This is the genuine rough outline of one of Spadger Island's stories.) With racist claptrap like this, it still seems amazing, in retrospect, that it took another 4 decades before British culture managed to ditch such calumnies as the *Black & White Minstrel Show*. Spadger was light relief against the *Wizard's* rugged heroes such as the athletic Alf Tupper, the 'tough of the track' and the intriguing Amazing Wilson, a character who had been born 'sometime in the 18th century', was over 150 years old, and lived wild on the Yorkshire moors wearing only a knitted wool tracksuit. Apart from his many other courageous deeds, he even managed to spend some time thrashing the Nazis as a pilot in the RAF.

The *Hotspur* was equally packed with imperial superiors, but with less pictures, as the bulk of the stories appeared in text. There was a public school ambience, with such stories about the Red Circle, with its school 'houses' such as the 'Conks'. At this school they studied subjects we'd never heard of and they even had something called 'Prep', with teachers like Mr. Goof, and characters named Alfred Smugg, Weepie Willie, Busty Parker and the class cheat and wag, Cribber, who issued such stock-in-trade threats as "I'll flatten you, you little rat!" The military featured heavily too, with The Wolf of Kabul, an English undercover officer fighting in Afghanistan *(plus ça change)* with his oriental sidekick, Chung, who appeared to have been armed solely with a cricket bat which he named 'Klicki-Ba', with Chung making such declarations as

"Klicki-Ba ... he like to smash skulls, master..." What better way to beat the crap out of Johnnie Foreigner than with a finely varnished slab of good old English willow?
Yes, some of Gilbert's stiff-upper-lip comics made my *Eagle* and *Film Fun* read like early editions of *Pravda*. There wasn't so much choice for girls, but the year after the *Eagle* first appeared, they brought out a sister publication called *Girl*. I remember trying to read a copy which Barbara brought to the den. It had stories no boy would touch; nurses, ballerinas, young women in peril abroad where nasty, dusky Arab types (Gad, Carruthers, *we* know what *they're* after!) were always lurking on the dockside, and a weekly feature entitled *Mother Tells You How* with such invigorating dialogue as;
Girl: "Oh, Mother, I do hope my new rug won't get dirty too quickly."
Mater: "I'll show you how to spray it so that it won't." At least, as lads, we had the comfort of knowing that with Dennis the Menace around, there wouldn't be a clean rug in the house.

One Saturday morning we were all sitting in the den studying something particularly exciting. My sea-going Uncle Laurie, a hard-drinking bosun in Hull's Ellerman's Wilson Line, had a friend who was on the New York route. He had brought some American comics back, and the one Laurie gave me featured an illustrated account of Custer's Last Stand. This had a colourful pictorial centre spread in the form of a map of the Battle of Little Big Horn. After we'd absorbed all the fine detail about Custer, and the activities of his more sensible officers, Major Marcus Reno and Captain Frederick Benteen, a plan began to form in my addled little mind. We could stage this battle on the golf course. As I closed the comic, there was a shower of hawthorn leaves and into our midst dropped a golf ball. I picked it up and peered out onto the course, where a squat old man in ice-blue trousers was standing, iron in hand, and looking puzzled. It was an excuse for me to make an appearance. As I stumbled out onto the soft green lawn, the man's caddy nudged his master and pointed at me. I held up the golf ball.

"Is this your ball, mister?"

The man in the blue pants marched forward with his hand out.

"Yes, son. Glad you found it – it's a Titliest."

What did he say, I thought – a '*tit* light?'

"I thought it was a golf ball."

"Yes, lad, it is – the best golf ball in the world. Champions play with Titleist balls." He took the ball from me and turned to his caddy.

"Benny, give this lad a tanner for being honest." Looking slightly annoyed, the Caddy fished in his pockets and produced a shiny sixpence which he dropped into my open hand. This was *some* result!

The stocky character looked me up and down.

"Do you live near here?" I nodded.

"Well, we're often losing balls up this end of the links. I bet if you look around long enough in that hedge or the long grass, you'll find a few. If you do, any of the chaps playing will give you threepence a time for'em."

"Thanks very much, mister. But is it still sixpence for tit light balls?"

Growling under his breath, the caddy jammed an iron into the golf bag and glowered at me.

"Don't push your luck son. Now *sod off.*"

As I ambled back to the den, as my friends were out of earshot during this exchange, I had a great desire to tell them of my good fortune. Then common sense got the better of me. If they all knew about the golf balls they'd be all over the place looking for them. In a rare lurch into despicable capitalist character, I decided that those threepences were going to be all mine.

6: HIGH PLAINS GRIFTER

'One does not sell the earth upon which the people walk.'
CRAZY HORSE

'But there's nowt wrong with selling them their balls."
UNCLE CHARLIE.

We had experienced a wonderful event not long after moving into Wymersley Road. I had a new little brother, Alexander Edward. For the first few weeks he cried a lot, but once he'd started crawling he seemed OK. He had a lovely head of curly blonde hair, and Mam and Dad were very proud of him. Not long after Alexander's arrival we got a new dog, Major. He was a very friendly Labrador, passed onto us by Dad's brother, Fred, who had immigrated to Canada. Major was a much-loved member of the family, a fearless guard, although we were never sure how old he was. We also had a green budgie called Tommy, who used to play football with a ping-pong ball on our dining table. He could recite the whole of 'Pop Goes the Weasel' if you waved some millet or a cuttlefish at him. Finally, there was our cat, Ginger, a chunky old Tom who spent much of his time outdoors on long adventures, turning up about three times a week with yet another part of his tatty anatomy in shreds. Considering our fraught financial state, with Dad's less than spectacular wages, we were running quite a menagerie.

The nights were drawing in and one evening we were sitting around the table ready for our tea. Middle class readers please note; in our little proletarian world, there were three meals; breakfast, dinner (that was at mid-day) and what you call dinner we called 'tea'. I think even posher folk might call a meal after 6 pm 'supper', but that's another story.

The food we ate in those days would have made 'if it moves, fry it' chefs like Hugh Fearnley Whittingstall or Heston Blumenthal proud. Anyone else with an interest in medical health matters would, upon seeing our abattoir-inspired table, have been carried away jibbering in horror on a stretcher. The idea of steak was eternally out of the question. That was the kind of thing you'd eat if you'd won the pools, or were requesting your last meal before they hung you in the morning. Chicken only appeared (and then, only if we could afford it) at Christmas, and Turkey was simply a country in the Middle East.

In the main, we ate offal. In those days there were tripe shops in Hull, and just around the corner from Beverley Road, I think at the corner of Marlborough Terrace, there was still a horsemeat shop. As Dad had a residual affection for horses after his stint in India, we never descended as low as Dobbin stew. But anything else was game. Tripe and onions was a regular fixture on the Bainton menu. I think we ate mainly sheep tripe, but if you're curious at this stage, here's a definition; Beef tripe is usually made from only the first three chambers of a cow's stomach: the rumen (blanket/flat/smooth tripe), the reticulum (honeycomb and pocket tripe), and the omasum (book/bible/leaf tripe). It was boiled in milk with onions, and sometimes fried (with onions), and the fried version we used to sprinkle with vinegar. The latter recipe used to inspire a sense of longing when one of us felt hungry during the day, resulting in culinary-inspired ramblings such as "Eee – I could eat a plate of tripe – wi'vinegar in every hole...". Apparently, the term 'offal' has Germanic, Scandinavian and Dutch origins – roughly translated it means 'garbage', or, 'off-fall' – anything which falls to the ground during the butchering of an animal. I would often come home from school and find some poor animal's head looking at me from the draining board. Mam's favourite gag was that she always addressed the butcher with 'Give us a sheep's head – and leave the eyes in – it'll see us through the week'. Eat your heart out, Ked Dodd.

The most popular were pig's heads, with sheep running a close second. The pig's head was extremely versatile. We even ate the ears. There was a lot of meat on a pig's cheeks, and other scrapings were utilised to make brawn. (An old English word for 'head cheese'). These assorted bits of shaved-off pork were cooked then placed in a basin and set in gelatine. The resulting brawn would be sliced up cold for tea. Pig's trotters were a regular delicacy, and when we had a sheep's head we often ate the brains, although even in those days having to force that slippery substance down my gullet almost made me retch. The finest offal, though, was beef heart. A cow's heart was the size of a football and there wasn't an ounce of waste on it. Either boiled or roasted, it sliced beautifully and there always seemed plenty of it. Occasionally we had chitterlings, which were intestines stuffed with mashed potato and fried. Ox tongue was usually reserved for Sunday tea, (although the idea of eating something which had been in a cow's mouth did give me trouble) and there was one particular part of an animal which my Mam called 'cow's ure' but I'm convinced it was the pancreas, which comes under the heading 'sweetbreads'.

Of course, with the city's fishing industry at its zenith, cod and haddock were often served, but Mam could even economise there, too. She went for a fish called Coley, which looked rather beige and discoloured when raw, but when you fried it up it was as white as any haddock. If we were ever in town Mam would visit the Monument Fisheries shop, next door to Ferens' Art Gallery on Monument Bridge. She never descended to the class-conscious depths of the snootier lady fish customers, who would always add to their request for 'three pounds 'of coley' with 'it's for the cat'. Looking back that was a small enclave of show business history, because the

fishmonger knew my Mam, and he was brother to the strangulated tenor, David Whitfield, who would go on to have 18 chart hits between 1953 and 1958. Don't ask me why; to me he always sounded like a bloke with his nuts in a vice, or wearing a truss with a spike in it. And two doors from
Monument Fisheries was the tailor's shop run by Morrie Lipman, whose daughter, Maureen, would one day become star of stage and screen. One final delicacy was the ham shank. Right up until her premature death at the age of 58 in 1973, Mam would often buy a couple of ham shanks, (always very cheap), boil them up, then cut all the fat off and salvage the remaining lean meat. This would be put through a table-top Spong mincer. Now, if you're unfamiliar with this device, it was *not* something invented by Spike Milligan for the *Goon Show*. The Spong Mincer was real – in fact, a 1952 survey by Mass Observation established that two thirds of Britain's households possessed a Spong. Today, they're a collector's item on e-Bay. I digress. The boiled ham shards would go through the Spong, followed by potatoes and onions. Then the whole lot would be mixed together in a big bowl with a few handfuls of flour and a couple of eggs. It was then formed into patties and deep fried. Delicious; probably 600 calories a mouthful, and that's why today I'm still built like a cross between Sir Cyril Smith and the later Orson Welles.

Anyway, on the day in question, we were enjoying a genuine treat – rabbit pie. It contained two rabbits Dad had managed to snare in the embankment near the golf course. As the last bit of delicious crust dissolved on my palate, I thought it time to see if my knowledgeable father knew anything about the bizarre goings-on on the golf course.

"Dad ... what's golf? Can *you* play it?"
He sucked the meat off a rabbit bone then wiped his mouth.
"Rich man's game. No, I can't play it, and neither do I want to."
"Where did it come from? Is it a new game?"

"No. Goes back thousands of years. The Chinese invented it and the Romans, I think, used to play it. Silly lark if you ask me. Golfers are lazy people with more money than sense. What kind of sport is it that has you wandering about all day looking for a little ball while you try and do arithmetic in your head? It's just an excuse to do business deals dressed as a clown – that's why it's expensive. First you have to be a member of a club, then there's the equipment – them irons and woods, the clubs, aren't cheap, and I don't know why, but have you seen the stupid clobber they wear? Crikey, can you imagine me in some of that get-up?" I looked at him. No, he was right. He looked OK in his overalls or his only suit – still his demob suit – and his trilby hat. But he certainly wasn't the golfing type.

"I wonder what the Roman golfers used to wear," I pondered.

"Sandals and little leather skirts," said Dad.

"Do you think they had tit light balls?"

Dad placed his knife and fork on the table, reached over with a long, muscular arm, clouting me across the cheek with a hand the size of a dinner plate. My face stung. I was shocked.

"We'll do without that sort of language, young man!" he barked.

"No," I wailed, "a man on the golf course said that tit light balls were the best in the world..."

Mam and Dad exchanged glances.

"Mmm, *did he*, now? What did he mean by that then?"

"It's the name on the golf ball – it isn't rude. The name of the people who makes the balls. When I find one, I'll show you it – honest."

"I should hope so," he smiled, as Mam leaned across and playfully ruffled my hair. I think he realised that clouting me one was a mistake, because what came next was a pleasant surprise.

"Right. I've told you about golf. Now you tell me something about Crazy Horse." This was my chance to show off. I took a deep breath.

"He used to wear a pebble tied behind his ear. And his hair was different to the other Indians. Lighter. They called him 'Curly' when he was young. He killed a buffalo before he was twelve. His dad was called Crazy Horse, but gave Curly his own name and then had a new name himself – so his dad became 'Worm'. Crazy Horse didn't take scalps. He never wore a full war bonnet, just one red hawk feather, and his war paint was a lightning flash across his face, and he painted his body with white dots like hailstones."

"Was he a good soldier?" asked Dad.

"He was a brave and a warrior. That's like a soldier, isn't it?"

Dad sat back, rolling a cigarette. He lit up and blew out a cloud of smoke.

"Aye, I suppose so. He gave that Custer a kicking."

Our immediate next door neighbours were an oddball family. The Nellists were an elderly couple with two adult sons. We rarely saw Mr. and Mrs. Nellist, but their sons, John and Joe, big, lumbering Boris Karloff types, could be heard thudding off along the path in their heavy boots to work at around 7.30 every morning. We never discovered what work they did, but I'm sure it must have been something like killing animals in a slaughterhouse. They had that look about them. John was the intelligent one; well, not exactly Einstein, but you could have some kind of conversation with him. Joe, slightly more muscular and cave-man like, was what we kids regarded as a 'looney'. Today we'd call him mentally challenged, or as having learning difficulties. Yet Joe Nellist, with his odd sadistic streak, fascinated us. When we were outside playing at weekends, he would often come out with his air pistol. Now, someone who had a real gun could gain our attention. It looked like a German Luger pistol, but it fired lead pellets. One day Joe called us over to the front door of their hut. To our horror, he'd used four drawing pins to pin a live frog to the door. He loaded his gun, and then with the deftness of a hungry chameleon, snatched a daddy longlegs from a nearby bush.

This insect was then rolled up and pushed down the barrel of the gun. We stood there, drop-jawed, as he grunted

"Hrrgh! Daddy longlegs in gun. Frog on door. Me kill frog with daddy longlegs." At that, he pulled the trigger and the poor twitching frog expired with an insect-filled hole in his ribcage. We all grimaced, stood back several steps exclaiming "Wooaah!" He turned and grinned, displaying a set of teeth one colour short of a snooker set.

The following day, I was sitting in the den in the hedge with Gilbert and our two school friends Billy and Lionel. Thankfully, Barbara wasn't there; it was Sunday and her family were churchgoers. Suddenly the ground seemed to quake as we felt the thud of hobnail boots approaching. Through the undergrowth the cadaverous, grinning visage of Joe appeared.

"Can me come in?" We daren't refuse him. He stumbled in and sat down on an old wooden beer crate. He looked at us.

"What doin'?"

"Talking," said Lionel.

"What 'bout?" asked Joe.

"Pictures," said Gilbert, "films – what's on at pictures."

Joe looked blank. The terms cineaste and psychotic frog-murderer do not sit well together. He sat staring into the middle distance for a while whilst we nervously awaited his next Neanderthal utterance. When it came, he surprised us.

"Wanna see a secret 'fing?" he asked. We all looked at one another. Better humour him.

"Yeah, alright..." said Billy, "what's that, then?"

To our horror arose to his full height, unbuttoned his fly and wopped out his prodigious penis. There was a communal sharp intake of breath. Bizarre though this was, for some peculiar reason we couldn't take our eyes off the thing. It was enormous; a wrinkle-headed pale pink saveloy with a dark blue vein down the side. He jiggled it around, making a snuffly, giggling sound somewhere in the back of his mouth.

"You wanna touch it?"

A paranoid falsetto chorus of "No thanks!" rang out.

"Me see *your* willies?"

Another collective, negative vocal response, expelled on a gust of nervous breath. He walked around a few paces, flapping the gargantuan mutton truncheon near our faces, then thankfully, tucked it away and fastened his buttons, to a loud sigh of relief from us. He turned to leave.

"Go have dinner now. Sausages." And then he was gone.

The rest of our conversation had no connection to the cinema whatsoever.

At tea time that night, potted beef sandwiches, followed by jelly and custard, Mam asked me what I'd been up to during the afternoon.

"Bet you've been playing cowboys and Indians again, eh?"

I wasn't sure whether I should mention the anatomy lesson provided by our primeval visitor, but there was something slightly worrying about it, and it seemed a good idea to get my parents' take on such an event.

"Big daft Joe came in our den this afternoon," I said. Dad had been sitting quietly smoking a roll-up but now his interest was aroused. He looked at me through narrowed eyes.

"What did that big twerp want, coming into your den?"

"He showed us his willie," I said. A mouthful of strawberry blancmange fell out of Mam's mouth and plopped onto the tablecloth. Dad inhaled too quickly on his fag and began coughing and spluttering. He gathered his composure and stubbed out his cigarette. Gripping the edge of the table with both of his huge hands, he leaned in towards me. I was terrified. There was something dark and threatening in his face; I had to remind myself that this was a man who had fought in the jungle and killed people.

"Tell me that again..." he said, slowly and evenly.

"Joe showed us his willie."

"What else?"

I looked baffled.

"Come on! What else did he do?!"

"Well ... he asked us if we wanted to touch it and then he wanted to see ours."

"And *did* you?"

"No – we *didn't!*" I wailed.

Dad rarely swore, and wasn't given to profanity, but this was an exception.

"Christ on a *bike!* The *dirty* bugger!"

At that, he got up and left the room. We heard the front door slam.

Mam sat quietly feeding Alexander with a bottle as I stroked the dog. We didn't speak, but Mam glanced at me wearing an expression of abject pity as she quietly 'tut-tutted' under her breath. Twenty minutes passed, then the front door opened and closed and Dad entered again, sat back at the table and rolled a fresh ciggie. He was shaking slightly and stared at the tablecloth through half closed eyes. Nothing more was said; an hour later I was in bed, and drifted off into a deep sleep.

It was after five pm the following day. I was playing outside with my catapult when I heard the sound of Joe arriving home along the concrete path. But this time his boot steps had an odd rhythm; clunk, scrape, clunk, scrape. Then I saw him. He was limping along, and looked as if he'd been rogered by a gorilla and run over by a centurion tank. His nose was broken, patched up with a large elastoplast. He shot a brief grin at me before going into his hut, and his front teeth had gone. He was covered in bruises with a real shiner of a black eye. Needless to say, we never saw much of him again, and he never visited us in the den.

I had three serious projects to occupy me. One, due to my increasing infatuation with Barbara Addison, was to convince her that, contrary to my lack of ability in the cycling department, that I still possessed the scientific sophistication to be a spaceman. (At that point the term 'astronaut' had not entered common parlance.) To do this, in addition to my continuing studies of the Sioux, I had started looking into the possibilities of Space Travel. For Christmas one of my presents was something called, (approximately) *The Boy's Big Book of Space.* There were several weird stories in it. One concerned a plot to attack various places on the face of the earth by putting huge mirrors into orbit and reflecting and intensifying the rays of the sun, and aiming them, the same way you could do on terra firma with a pocket mirror, at targets, giving their inhabitants something a bit more serious than a touch of sunburn. In some ways it must have been an early precursor of Ronald Reagan's *Star Wars* device. Yet at the end of this big, fascinating soft-back pulp publication, there were some addresses one could write to. One was The British Interplanetary Society in London. This was very exciting. A society interested in space travel? I had to have some of that. So, I wrote them a letter, asking some questions about did they think there was life on other planets, and how fast would a spaceship have to travel to escape the pull of earth's gravity. Two weeks passed and I got a typed reply on the Society's headed notepaper. Now, *this* was going to impress Barbara! Yes, they did believe there might be people on other planets – possibly Venus. And how fast would a rocket have to travel to escape earth? This was something called the 'escape velocity'. It was, apparently, 7.6 miles per second. The letter was signed by someone called Arthur C. Clarke, and I wish I still had it.

My second project, as junior wholesaler of lost golf balls, was going well. Every two days, after school, I would go out onto the golf course and search diligently through the long grass around the perimeter, and some days I'd find as many as six balls. About every ten days, I'd put these into a brown paper carrier bag and set up shop by the Hawthorn hedge. Several golfers got to know me, and at three pence a time (3d, probably about 1.5p in new money) I was impressively supplementing my half crown (12.5p) weekly pocket money. Although Dad admired my entrepreneurial adventure, he did say something odd one night when I came in with a golf ball income of about four shillings and sixpence in my pocket.

"You know what the American gangsters call people like you?" he asked. "No – what?" I said, shaking my head.

"A grifter."

I looked puzzled.

"What's a grifter?" I enquired.

"Well, on American fairgrounds, he's a kind of confidence man, somebody who tricks you out of your money."

"But I'm not tricking nobody," I argued, "if they lose their balls, and I find them, then they pay me threepence a time."

I looked at Mam for support. I was very concerned.

"Am I a …a 'grifter', Mam?"

She was changing Alexander's pungent nappy.

"No, son. But I bet all those chaps out there on the golf course are."

My third, and premier project remained, of course, Crazy Horse. I was now adept at making bows and arrows, a task which had been helped by Dad's carpentry skills. And although it would seem a totally irresponsible act by a parent in today's Health and Safety world, Mam had bought me a more or less 'professional' metal catapult from Dinsdale's Joke Shop in Hull's Hepworth Arcade.

None of these time-consuming diversions did much to aid my flagging prowess as a student at school. I was good at art, (considered to be a useless skill in and industrial society) and shone at English, (only marginally behind art in terms of parental respect) with my fanciful compositions about space and Indians always earning top marks. But in everything else I was a laughing stock and no more so than in arithmetic. In pre-calculator days we were actually expected to use our brains to add and subtract. In order to strengthen this academic muscle, we were made to learn, by rote, our multiplication tables. I dreaded those lessons which came under the heading 'sums', because maths teachers (and this is a conclusion which remained with me for the next 8 years) were, in the main, out and out sadists. They liked nothing better than picking on the dumbest kid in an arithmetic class (always me) and barking "Stand on your chair! Recite the 7-times table!" Two twos are four, great. Even five fives are twenty five – easy. But sevens and nines or sixes ... I still shudder. In later childhood, as will be seen, when I entered the no-man's land of algebra and geometry, with its nasty relatives logarithms, cosines and tangents, the goose of my life was well and truly cooked.

I was also an utter dunce at anything to do with physical education and sports. I did have a brief flirtation with football, however. The strip at Wold Road School was green shirt, with white and green striped socks. I think it was Dad's influence, upon me showing an interest in the game, which propelled him during a period when he'd earned some extra money from copious overtime at work, to forego paying the outstanding bill to the coal man in order to buy me a Wold Road Juniors soccer kit, complete with boots and shin pads. I have no recollection of how it happened, but I had stayed behind on some occasions when the sports teacher was supervising trials for the team. I had little hope of being selected, but fully fitted out in my new togs I stood on the touchline watching a vicious tackle by a big lad from the class above mine. With his nigh-on crippled little victim lying face down in the mud, the teacher blew his whistle, brought the fowler of and gave me a sidelong glance.

"What's your name, boy?"

"Roy Bainton sir."

"Right – on you go, let's see what you can do."

Although I scored no goals and had absolutely no idea what position I was playing, I managed to run around energetically in the manner of a grounded fly minus its wings, and even made a few decent passes. When the game finished, the teacher gathered us all in a bunch at the side of the pitch and announced that on the coming Saturday morning there would be a match between Wold Road Juniors and a school from a street off Hull's Chanterlands Avenue, the name of which escapes me. He read out the team and, to my surprise, included my name.

I would be playing on something called 'the wing'. When I got home that night I was surprised to find my Uncle Charlie there, paying us a visit. I was still in my muddy football gear, with my school clothes in a brown paper carrier. When I told everyone that I'd been selected for the Saturday match, Dad was impressed and Charlie gave me a kind of slow handclap.

"Now then. A bit of football – that's the stuff to give the troops. Better than all that Crazy Horse stuff, bows and arrows and space ships, eh?"

I loved Uncle Charlie but I had to vehemently disagree.

"Just because I'm playing football doesn't mean I can't be Crazy Horse and Dan Dare," I said.

Charlie threw his head back and laughed.

"You'll grow out of all that rhubarb," he said, "and anyway, let's face it, lad - you'll never be an Indian as long as you've got a hole in your arse ... there's no future in it."

Dad looked askance at Charlie.

"Now then, Chas – you're not on the docks now. Watch your language!"

I went to bed that night feeling slightly disappointed with Charlie, even though he'd given me half a crown before he left. He might know all about dockers and the Klondyke Café, and sure, he made me laugh and looked after the Old Vinegar Bottle, but he knew nothing about being a Sioux.

The game on that Saturday against the visiting team was my first and final foray into the world of association football. It's a wonder I left the playing field alive. In the first twenty minutes of the first half, I'd managed to score two home goals. I was as popular as a fart in a space suit. The taunts went on for weeks; "Oh, here he comes – the Own Goal Kid ..." I never wore my football kit ever again, much to my parents' disappointment. Anyway, we sold it to my better-off classmate, Gilbert.

Crazy Horse and The Coalman

7: CUSTER COPS IT

When I was a boy, the Sioux owned the world. The sun rose and set on their land; they sent ten thousand men to battle. Where are the warriors today? Who slew them? Where are our lands? Who owns them?

Sitting Bull

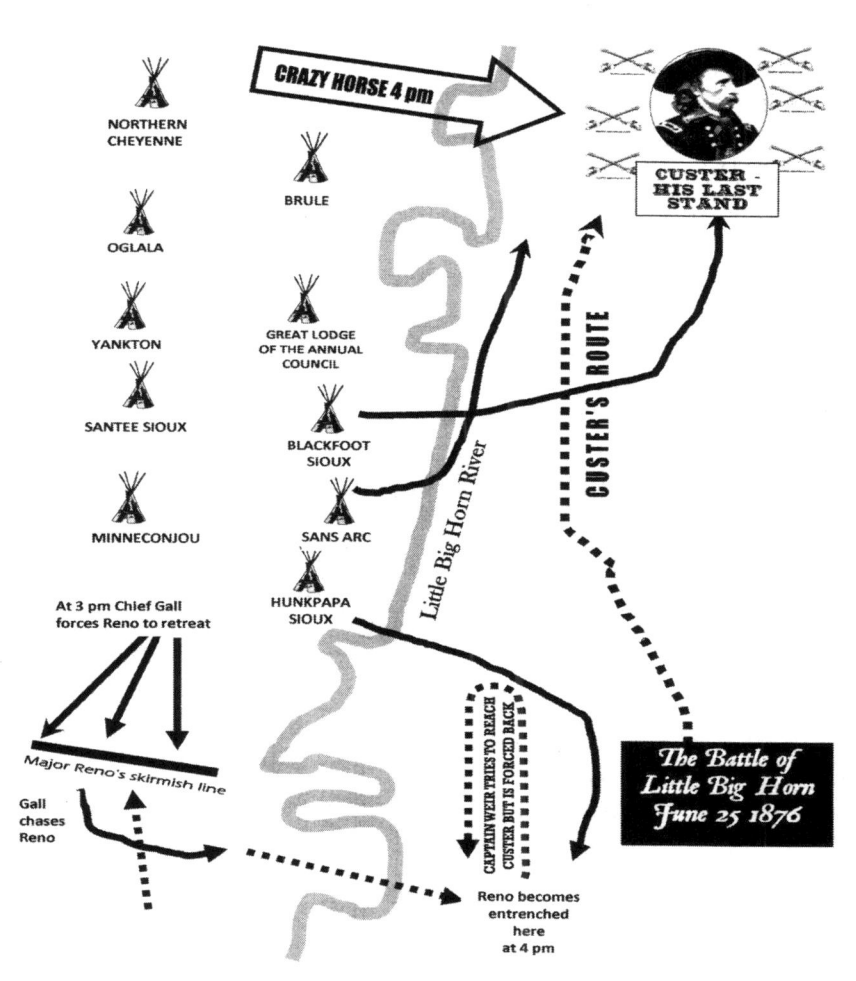

[Map: The Battle of Little Big Horn, June 25 1876, showing Northern Cheyenne, Brule, Oglala, Yankton, Great Lodge of the Annual Council, Santee Sioux, Blackfoot Sioux, Minneconjou, Sans Arc, Hunkpapa Sioux encampments along the Little Big Horn River; Crazy Horse 4pm arrow; Custer - His Last Stand; Custer's Route; At 3pm Chief Gall forces Reno to retreat; Major Reno's skirmish line; Gall chases Reno; Captain Weir tries to reach Custer but is forced back; Reno becomes entrenched here at 4pm]

As Autumn began to fade into winter in 1951 three exciting things happened. First, together with Gilbert, Lionel and Billy and two other lads from the nearby gypsy encampment,

I fulfilled my plan to stage the Battle of the Little Big Horn on the golf course.

It took place on a chilly Saturday afternoon, at the same time as the real battle, between 3 and 4 pm. Needless to say, with our limited resources, history was not reproduced all that accurately and the original 1876 participants may have had more serious problems than being interrupted by a succession of angry golfers threatening to have us expelled. Yet we persevered. I had planned it all out in an exercise book. I and the two gypsy lads would represent the three main Indian attacks; the Sioux Chief Gall to the south to attack Major Reno, (Billy) at 3 pm, then Gall's Blackfeet and Sans Arc forces would break into the north-east where Custer (Gilbert) had been heading whilst Reno was being attacked. Lionel would have the final manoeuvre as Captain Benteen, who reached Reno's position at 4.30, by which time, in the north, Custer had fought his last. But Lionel's Benteen was only allowed to reach Billy's Reno after I, as Crazy Horse, had attacked Custer from the north-west and totally destroyed his forces (represented by Gilbert). Our 'cavalry' were armed with cap pistols whilst I (of course) had a bow and arrows and the gypsy lads had bamboo war lances decorated with pigeon feathers. (I had one tied around my head with a length of Mam's knicker elastic.) I tried to persuade my 'braves' to bring one of the encampment's horses, just for an added touch of authenticity, but the response I got from the Gypsy elder, Cyril, bordered on a Romany curse, so I gave up. We did have something the Sioux might have had, though – Major, our dog, found the whole event much to his liking, and ran around all over the place barking, much to the anger of the occasional golfer who stopped to remonstrate with us. It was almost dark when we finished at 4.45 pm.

    To allay battle fatigue, we retired to the den for that well-known Sioux victory feast of the plains, sausage rolls and Dandelion & Burdock. As ever, I had to dismiss Gilbert's constant complaints about the two garden cane arrows I fired hitting him in a sensitive place.

It was very cold that winter. The second thing to happen when the clocks changed and the nights drew in was something far less important. There was a General Election. Mam and Dad were always going on about somebody called Mr. Atlee, and we had various visits from people called 'candidates', Dad becoming quite stroppy with the Conservative. Anyway, Labour, despite the 1945 landslide, lost, and once again Winston Churchill became Prime Minister. The final result was Conservatives and Associates - 321 seats; Labour - 295; Liberal - 6; and others 3.

The third important thing to happen came in November, when Dad lost his job with the building firm, and had to start looking for more work. It was also a very difficult time because we'd built up quite a bill with the coal man and although we all hid in darkness when he came to deliver one night, just after tea, this time he refused to let us have the coal and shouted through the letter box,

"I know you're all in there. You owe me four pounds seven and six. If you want your coal next week, get ready to pay me summat!" At that he was gone. Eventually, Mam put the lights on and we sat by the fire. Mam shed a tear as Alexander crawled around the room, burbling.

"We've only got enough coal for tomorrow," she said. Dad consoled her by saying there were plenty of trees in the area and he'd go and chop wood, but we all knew that wasn't the answer. It had been noted, however, that there was an answer, although it required a degree of illegality to make it work.

The main road at the junction of Wold Road and Wymersley Road was a large triangular area where the EYMS bus service turned around and terminated. A few days earlier, Hull Corporation Council had arrived there and set up a wheeled workman's lobby, which would be a shelter and base for road workers during the day, whilst at night it would house a watchman. The crew's task over the coming weeks was to totally re-tarmac the area.

The lobby was the size of a railway goods wagon, with small windows and a metal chimney stack. Above all, workers who spent their time outdoors in those days had to have their breaks and lunches in warmth and comfort, with plenty of hot tea. This meant a large stove, kept glowing by gas coke. We were all familiar with coke. We even had it delivered sometimes as an alternative to ordinary coal, because it was far less smoky and gave off a fierce, glowing heat. I had noticed, as had the rest of the family, that a veritable mountain of this fine fuel, probably a couple of tons, had been piled up in the open air at the roadside at the rear of the watchman's lobby. As a road safety measure, the mountain's perimeter was marked off at night with a series of glowing red oil-lamps.

Dad sat looking into our fading fire, and then looked across at Mam.

"Tell you what. I could nick some of that coke across the road."

Mam caught her breath and shook her head.

"Oh, aye – and you'd get caught, then the Council would take you to court, you'd be in the *Hull Daily Mail* as a criminal – try and get a job *then* …"

"I could do it quiet. Nobody would know. Leave it till late."

"No!" barked Mam. "You'll get prosecuted. You'll be seen."

They sat pondering for a few moments then Dad looked my way, smiling. I was sitting at the table, making a spaceship with corrugated cardboard, silver paper and egg shells. Dad started talking whilst looking straight at me, but he was really addressing Mam.

"Ah, now then. I could get prosecuted, but the lad couldn't. He's only eight, so he'd just get a telling off from the Bobbies."

Mam closed her eyes and lowered her head. I suppose she felt slightly ashamed at what she'd just heard, and more so because Dad was right, although the possibility of me being

inveigled into the role of Artful Dodger did make me look at Dad with Fagin in mind.
But Mam didn't like it.
"So, we have to make our lad into a crook to keep warm."
"No, no! He'll be OK - they'd think he was larking about!"
He turned to me again.
"Y'think you could go on a night time mission, eh, lad?"
The way he put it made it sound vaguely exciting.
"What would I have to do?"
"There's two buckets round the back in the garden. We'll let you stay up nice and late, past nine o'clock, you could go over the road, and really, really quietly, fill the buckets with coke and bring them home. It's not far, and coke isn't as heavy as coal."

The 'mission' was at first terrifying. Dad had given me careful instructions about what to say in the event of being caught. I was to tell whoever apprehended me that I felt sorry for my Mam and Dad because they hadn't any coal, and that I'd come across the road myself to try and help them. It was nothing to do with them.
It was bitterly cold and there was frost on the ground, but fortunately there was no moon. The door to the lobby was closed but there was a light burning inside and smoke coming from the chimney. Crouched on the icy kerb, I began filling the first bucket. Dad said I couldn't use a shovel because it would make a noise, so I rummaged with both hands in the coke to find the biggest pieces. Filling both buckets took me fifteen minutes. Contrary to my Dad's suggestion, my cargo was damned heavy, but eventually I reached home and he was waiting, with a lit candle in a jam jar, and met me at our coal bunker, into which we tipped the coke in as quietly as possible.
"Now," he said, "that didn't take too long, did it?"

I had a bad feeling about what was to come next. I was right.
"Tell you what – nip across and get some more."

All in all, I made three trips that night, and repeated the exercise every night for the following week. On the final night, I was halfway home when the handle came off one of the buckets. The contents spilled out onto the path. It had made quite a noise and I froze in the darkness as I watched the door to the lobby open and the night watchman come out and walk around his domain with a torch, but within minutes he was back inside, the door slammed and bolted. I sighed with relief. Eventually Dad came and helped me pick up the coke and we managed to have small yet decent fires for a few days, which Dad supplemented by sawing some logs from a tree at the end of our garden.

The following week Dad was awarded a brotherly distress grant from the Royal Antediluvian Order of Buffaloes. Like most of the older adults in the family, including sea-going uncles, Dad had been a 'Buff' since he was old enough to join at 18. I used to think it had some connection to the Indians, what with it involving buffaloes, but when I was initiated into the sect myself at the Half Way House pub on Hessle Road the age of 18, I realised it was a bargain-basement version of the Freemasons for poor folk, providing hen-pecked working men with an 'official' excuse to go out for a pint. However, their generosity and solidarity in having a whip-round for Dad meant that we managed to pay the coal man, and after ten days of fire rationing, we once more had a good blaze to keep us warm.

Dad was only out of work for just under a month, and was extremely fortunate to land a much better job than the one he'd lost.

He was a good joiner and carpenter with a good reputation. He was to become a shuttering foreman on a site in Hull City Centre, where they were erecting new shops to replace those bombed during the '39-'45 unpleasantness. Although Christmas was approaching fast, when he got his first wages he bought Mam a present – a vacuum cleaner.

This lurch into the world of new domestic technology was an exciting event for me. In my constant zeal for impressing Barbara Addison, I had become adept at making cardboard space ships with the tubes from Izal toilet rolls with egg shells as nose-cones. In order to simulate blast-off, I would attach a long length of black cotton to my interplanetary craft and throw this over the open beams in the living room. Then, following count-down, I would pull the cotton and my pre-NASA Apollo would ascend to the heavens, or at least to the ceiling beams.

It's worth pausing here for a digression on the nature of Izal toilet paper. Toilet paper in our house was a sporadic luxury item. In any case, if truth be told, we all preferred the regular working class toilet tissue of multiple 8-inch squares of the *Daily Mirror* or the *Express,* looped onto a piece of string and hanging on a nail on the lavvy door. At least newsprint, despite the ink stains on your underpants, is absorbent. The reason we had any Izal paper at all was that if Mam and Dad went to any toilets in town where they had it, they would nick it and bring it home. Izal seemed utterly unsuitable for bum-wiping. All it wiped was the smile off your face. It had the consistency of tracing paper (and made good tracing paper, too) with a slight gloss to it, yet it was impregnated with the disinfected odour of a Crimean war hospital. There were two types of Izal, the packaging of which was emblazoned with a green cross, to give it that 'medical' appeal. One was on rolls, and there was the posher version, in a box, where you pulled out individual sheets through a slot. Half a century on, one might have hoped that the EEC might have banned its use under the Geneva Conventions, but I noticed recently in a supermarket that it still exists, so there must still be a Spartan element of the British public walking around with unclean, sore arses.

But back to the vacuum cleaner. Dad arrived home with it one night from work. It was in a three-foot long cardboard box about ten inches square. The box bore the legend 'Vactric' and

I was keen to see it revealed but Dad made sure we'd all had our tea first, because this was an important event. Up until this glorious day, in a time long before the notion of fitted carpets,

Mam would collect up the home-made rag rugs each day and throw them over the washing line in the garden, where they would receive a thorough whacking with a carpet beater. Any dust in the house would be painstakingly swept up with a sweeping brush and collected with a dustpan and brush. It could be backbreaking work.

With the pots washed and everything cleared away, we sat in awe as Dad took the monster from its packaging. It was cylindrical, a metallic bottle green with glittering chrome fastenings and embellishments. Dad stood it on one end in front of the fire, and looked at me.

"Right, son – what does this remind you of?"

I knew it was a vacuum cleaner and that it was very important, so I hardly dare voice my thoughts. But Dad persisted.

"Come on – standing up on its end like this – what does it look like?"

I took a deep breath.

"A space rocket."

With some relief, I could see that I'd answered correctly. Dad beamed and nodded. Yes, all metallic green, with shiny fittings – all it needed was a windscreen and Dan Dare could pilot this – no problem. In fact, Dan Dare's personal spacecraft Anastasia, in the *Eagle,* was indeed metallic green. It made me realise that Mam and Dad must take more notice of my reading material than I thought if they'd bought a vacuum cleaner like this. An entertaining hour was spent attaching and re-attaching the tubes, brushes and accessories, but when Dad switched the thing on, it really did have that 'outer space' thing going for it, although Major the dog barked and Alexander started to cry.

Over the coming months, providing it wasn't plugged in, I was allowed to play spaceships with the Vactric every night. When you unfastened and removed the chrome cap at the suction end of the machine, it made a fine flying saucer. It was better than a Christmas present, both for me and Mam.

I can't recall what I got for Christmas that year. Alexander got a teddy bear and some toy cars – I think I mainly got books and a painting set. We had chicken for dinner, and Christmas pudding, a batch of which had been made by Mam and Dad way before in September, and stored in biscuit tins in the so-called 'meat safe', which was really a windowless stone-clad cupboard. We knew no-one wealthy enough to possess a refrigerator; such a device was years ahead for us.

In January it snowed and we all played on the golf course, but the snow played havoc with my golf ball business. As January 1952 drew to a close, the snow vanished and we were plunged into dark days of ivy fog. On the morning of February 6th I turned up for school, filled with anticipation, because that afternoon we would have our music lesson. This usually took the form of a class percussion band; tambourines, triangles, other instruments of a tuneless nature which escape me, but most importantly, drums. Only the chosen few got selected for the drums. After weeks of waiting, I thought that surely my day must have come. We were all standing in the assembly hall just after 9 am for morning prayers and the inevitable hymn. I remember that standing in the row in front of me were the Beezley twins; two 8 year old girls from a family who seemed even more destitute than ours. We were bad enough, with our sole footwear until Uncle Ken's next visit in the spring being well-worn wellingtons, which always chafed my bare legs. These were the decades when a boy's true rite of passage arrived around the age of 12 – that was when you were finally allowed to wear long trousers. I looked pityingly at the poor Beezley girls in their grubby little frocks and darned cardigans, when from the hem of one of their dresses appeared a large cockroach which slowly clambered its way up the folds of the cloth and disappeared into the back of her cardigan. It filled me with horror, and I counted my blessings. I'd rather

steal buckets of coke, I thought, than have to live their lives. There was a sombre air that morning in the hall.
The teachers looked more serious than usual, and the headmaster, Mr. Pickles, knocked his fist on the rostrum.

"Now then children. I don't know if some of you have heard on the radio, but today is a very sad day. Our beloved King George has died last night in his sleep, and the nation will be mourning. So, those of you whose parents are not out working can go home, as there will be no school today. Those of you whose mums and dads might be out can stay, and we will make other arrangements, and we will still be providing school dinners."

Damn! I thought – so much for my hopes for the drum this afternoon. The King is dead – God Bless the King – he's given us a day off, so we can do what we like.

And so, that afternoon, we went to the pictures. Mam loved the cinema. Just before Christmas she'd taken me to one of Hull's smallest (and quite the weirdest) cinemas, The Londesborough in Londesborough Street off Spring Bank. The film we saw has remained with me, indelibly fixed in my consciousness – the great Alistair Sim in *Scrooge*. It has remained part of our family Christmas for sixty years. On the day the King died, my friend Gilbert told me that his mother was crying about it when he got home. Being the lumpen lefties we were in our house (although Dad had a bit of military respect) there were no tears, because Mam had little time for the notion of Monarchy. This was the inevitable aftermath of a brief romance she had enjoyed just before the war, with a man called Jimmy, who was on the committee of the Hull Branch of the Communist Party. Mam told me once that Jimmy used to say

"Come the revolution, if we don't stand them all up against the wall and shoot the bloody parasites, we'll give 'em all a council house and the means test, just like the rest of us."

I had no thoughts in 1952 about the Royal Family one way or the other; they were just distant celebrities who appeared every now and then in the newspapers. As Mam commented, far better people died every day, but we never got to hear about it.

The King's death did put the mockers on everything, though. That day there was no *Worker's Playtime* on the radio, and they even took off my favourite, *Dick Barton, Special Agent*. Instead we had wall-to-wall sombre funeral music. Everybody seemed miserable and lots of women apparently had to go out to buy a black tie for their husbands.

I can't remember which cinema we went to, but the film was *Tom Brown's Schooldays*. As an exposition of the public school system it was quite chilling, and for me even more so, because it was about a strange system called '*boarding school*'. I wasn't sure what this meant, apart from the fact that boys were sent to such places not so much for education, but as some kind of long-term punishment, which included being away from your home and having to sleep in a dormitory with other boys. The whole notion of this was horrendous, and on the occasions when I ran foul of the family rules and misbehaved myself, then depending on the severity of my misdemeanour, 'boarding school' was the threat I faced. I recall one day being sent to the Co-operative shop on Wold Road to buy a loaf of bread. When I came home, as she always did, Mam pinched the loaf and declared it 'stale'. This meant I had to go back to the shop and ask for a fresh one. But the Co-op had run out of white farmhouse loaves and all they had left was something called a milk loaf. When I arrived home with this, Mam, who had admittedly been having a hard time suffering from toothache, flew into a rage. I made the daft mistake of saying something to the effect that it was 'only a loaf' and that it wasn't my fault, but then it began. She clipped me violently around the ear, shouting

"Don't you *dare* answer me back! First you let the shop palm you off with yesterday's bread, then you come home with this –"

she picked up the soft, pallid loaf and squeezed it, then threw it onto the table – "this cotton wool bloody pap! How can I make your dad's packing up with this rubbish?"

Without thinking I managed to infuriate her further by uttering

"Well, *somebody* must eat it – there was loads of it in the shop!"

She grabbed me by the scruff of the neck and dragged me to my bedroom, threw me in, then followed, reaching up on the top of the wardrobe and throwing down a small, battered brown suitcase. She opened it on the bed

"Right. Get all your clothes packed in this case, because I'm taking you to boarding school. They'll show you how to behave! And you'll not come home until summer holidays! Now get packing! You've got t*en minutes*!"

As the bedroom door slammed shut I was suddenly engulfed by a wave of horror and abject self-pity. I'd rarely seen her this angry. With tears gushing down my cheeks, I stuffed vests, socks and underpants into the case, then folded some shirts, but the case was too small and I simply flopped onto the bed, sobbing.

What must have been ten minutes, but felt like an hour, passed as I lay with my face buried in my pillow. Then I heard the door open. I dared to look. Mam was standing there. First she looked at the suitcase and then at me, and to my surprise, she began to cry. She came over and sat by the bed, cradling me in her arms and stroking my hair.

"Oh, you daft lad. You daft, *daft* lad. Look how you make your poor Mam behave." It was a tender moment, but I was still worried.

"Am I going to boarding school?"

She dried her eyes on her apron and smiled.

"No, of course you're not. You don't want to live with all those snotty upper class twerps in a dormitory, do you?"

I was relieved. "No...no, I don't."

"Well be a good lad and don't upset your Mam. I'm not feeling very well and I can't be doing with all that backchat. When your Mam and Dad tell you to do things, it's for a reason. Remember, everything we do is for each other. And you have to learn these things – like just standing up for us when shops try and sell us stale bread, because they know you're a little rough kid and they think it doesn't matter. Always stand up for yourself and for your family. Now, put all those clothes back and come and have your tea."

The day the King died, that sombre, dark, foggy cold day, as the nation grieved, in the Priory Cinema I watched what could be my own fate if I misbehaved any more. Tom Brown being roasted by the fire by the evil Flashman. What kind of kids were these? Even my school's lousiest bully, Dick Cornick, would have stopped short at such behaviour. He might steal a sausage from your plate in school dinner time, but would he bake our junior flesh by an open fire? No – he wouldn't dare. It seemed that with boarding school, I'd had a narrow escape.

❖ ❖ ❖ ❖

Crazy Horse and The Coalman

8: INDIAN SUMMER

I am alone in the world. I want to live in these mountains; I do not want to go to Tularosa. That is a long way off. I have drunk of the waters of the Dragoon Mountains and they have cooled me: I do not want to leave here.

Cochise, Apache Chief.

As winter rolled into spring Mam's daily pain with her bad teeth was finally ended. She visited the dentist and had every tooth in her mouth removed. When she came home that day she looked terrible. She had a pasty, sallow pallor and was holding a large wad of blood-stained cotton wool to her mouth. Dad had arrived home early and was making the tea; beans on toast, but he soon realised that Mam could never tackle such a delicacy, and opened a tin of Heinz soup. Within a few weeks she would be fitted out with a sparkling set of pristine white dentures, and that day of her new smile was one of great joy, because I'd seen a toothless old cowpoke at the pictures every week called Gabby Hayes, and in Mam's toothless weeks, I couldn't help but make comparisons.

Staying at school for school dinners wasn't a regular thing for me. As school was only a ten minute walk, and we didn't have to be back before 1.30, unlike many kids I had the luxury, on days when Mam wasn't out, of being able to go home. It saved Mam sixpence (eventually nine pence) per day in dinner money, and as I always found school catering a depressing challenge, going home was a pleasant option, Each week, usually around Friday dinner time, we'd have a visit from Uncle Ken. I suppose he earned the title 'uncle' because we saw much more of him on a regular basis than real uncles.

Ken, as previously described, was a minor version of a loan shark. He worked for a furniture store in Hull city centre which had a profitable adjunct to the business of selling tacky kitchen cabinets, grotesque, badly made three piece suites and sewing machines – money lending.

Yet when it came to clothing for the family, his indispensible services never appeared as hard cash, but in the form of something called a 'club cheque' (known further north as a 'tally'). This could only be spent at a prescribed list of clothing shops that worked in partnership with Ken's employers, and got a rake-off from his deals via a small cut and some cash flow.

Our parents rarely bought new clothing. They seemed to make do with what they had for years. There was no 'fashion' statement to make among a struggling, post-war working class. As long as we had something to keep us dry and warm, what it looked like didn't matter. Of course, the middle classes liked to show off a little, and their kids at school always had the best pullovers and smart gabardine raincoats, as well as leather shoes. But in club cheque world, Mam had to make £10 go a long long way, and this usually meant the Army and Navy Stores. We had two forms of footwear to see us through the year. Spring and summer saw us in sandshoes – comply known outside Hull as plimsolls. With their crepe soles and rubber toe-caps, these canvass, lace-up delights were the harbingers of summer days. Come September, we got a pair of rubber wellingtons. Depending on the frequency of Uncle Ken's loans and the amount of debt we were in, if the sandshoes were delayed until June's school holidays, then our wellies would be cut down to make then into shoes. The Army and Navy Stores of our family's choice seemed a long way to go because it was situated in West Hull in the fish dock area on Hessle Road. It was run by an elderly, friendly Jewish couple, Mr. and Mrs. Shields. The Shields knew all their club cheque customers by name, but as I got older (as will be seen in a later chapter), I began to find their stock and the choice it offered to be very frustrating. I longed for that magical break-point after the age of eleven when I'd qualify for long trousers. I hated the grey, short flannel pants I had to wear day in, day out, with their buttons and braces. Beneath these was an economy measure of ex-army underpants cut down and taken in to fit boyish nether regions, and if you were particularly unlucky, ex-army vests. They itched like hell to the point where I wondered how the hell we'd ever won the war if our services had to suffer such sartorial irritation on top of bullets and bombs. Everything was buttoned. Zips back then were a level of sophistication still on the horizon. We usually got either a navy blue flannel blazer for school, which had to double up as 'best' for everything else, and the cheapest, flimsiest rain coat going. There would be a couple of sleeveless pullovers (I don't think the term 'tank top' came in until the 70s) which, when washed, usually did one of two things – it either stretched to the point of almost becoming a cocktail dress or it shrank halfway up your back. Then there were the cheap, itchy socks and scarves, and Torquemada's schoolboy revenge, the balaclava. Going to school in winter minus your balaclava was almost illegal. I suppose the IRA wear the damned things as a constant reminder of the grimness of their mission. In fact, the only small element of style I can recall prior to 1957 was the elastic belts we wore with a snake-shaped buckle.

The difficulty for our parents was that we were growing taller and larger each school term and this was a costly exercise for us, but a profitable one for Uncle Ken, which eventually propelled him from his Raleigh push bike in 1952 to a moped by 1956. By his retirement in 1963 he'd acquired a Mercedes and a detached house in Hull's own version of Beverly Hills, Kirkella. Yet Uncle Ken managed to get his dinner every working day from the poorest people. He would stand in the kitchen with his usurer's account books and leather money pouch laid out on the table, and sniff the air like one of the Bisto kids, saying something to my mother like

"Aaah – do I smell meat and taty pie?"

To which Mam, conscious of the fact we owed him the equivalent of Bolivia's Gross National Product, would say
"Aye, that's right, Ken. Would you like some?"
He never said no. Pie, peas, pot of tea, another handful of money and he'd be off to his next victim.

Shields's Army Stores was one of many similar establishments, especially popular with working men. Following the mass de-mobilization after World War 2, there was literally tons of army surplus on the market. The navy blue ex-army beret was challenging the trilby and the flat cap. Everything from hob-nailed army boots, beloved of 1950s building workers, back packs, kitbags, huge, weighty greatcoats, leather tabards, battledress jackets, itchy shirts, shorts, belts, socks – it was wall to wall khaki. Because of its victory-inducing utility, this clothing was going to be around for a long time, and we lads would not be able to shake it off until James Dean and Elvis came on the scene several years later. Depending upon which lower, poverty-stricken strata of the working class you came from, for most of us it meant going to school dressed as something like a cross between a Japanese admiral and Desert Rat, but without the medals.

Dad had been working on council house building for various contractors and would often tell us about the new houses, one of which we were guaranteed. He told us they had bathrooms, gardens and hot and cold water. He thought that there might be a good chance of us moving in before Christmas. Yet this didn't excite me as much as it should have. As the council house phase approached, I knew that my Wymersley Road idyll was slowly moving to a close. Would I see my friends any more? And what about Barbara? She had come around to my Crazy Horse fixation, and in our last enactment of Little Big Horn on April 1st, my ninth birthday, she had even agreed to be Tsunke Witco's wife, Black Buffalo Woman. I was going to miss her; the sheer thrill of kissing her in our den and under our kitchen table in the winter time.

It was an exciting time, those first few months of 1952. Gilbert's parents had bought a TV set, and I was invited around to see Princess Elizabeth declare her self to be the new Queen. The big event, the actual coronation, would have to wait a year. Sadly, the previous year, *Dick Barton, Special Agent,* had been taken off the BBC. But there was still excitement on the airwaves. At 7.15 pm each night Radio Luxembourg was broadcasting Dan Dare, Pilot of The Future. Oddly enough, the actor who had played Dick Barton on the BBC, Noel Johnson, now became Dan Dare – a seamless transition from one heroic role to another. Produced in London, the series was sponsored by Horlicks, and did suffer on light nights when the signal from Luxembourg was weaker. It played havoc with the plot. Dan Dare's announcer was British Pathe News's favoured voice-over, Bob Danvers-Walker and the great thing about Dane Dare is that he was played by former Dick Barton actor Noel Johnson. Dan's 'ee-by-gum' Yorkshire sidekick, Digby, was played by John Sharpe, Peabody by Anne Cullen, and the evil, massively green headed Mekon by Francis De Wolfe. Other parts were played by Kenneth Williams and another theatrical great, Ralph Richardson.

The great thing about the Radio Dan Dare was the Horlicks Spaceman's Club, which you could join for 6d and a label from a Horlicks jar. Club goodies included your Spacefleet Service Identity Card, a Dan Dare Tie, the all-important Spaceman's Club Badge, but above all, *The Spaceman's Club Handbook.* You could get a special Dan Dare cup from which to drink your Horlicks, and a periscope.

The handbook was endlessly fascinating. All kinds of facts about Dan and his friends, the story of the forming of Spacefleet, with an inventory of equipment and vessels. For a would-be spaceman, there was everything – even details of the planets and what their inhabitants were like.

However, whereas I hadn't given up on Crazy Horse and the Sioux, I began to realise that there was no more mileage in re-enacting his battles. I simply couldn't get enough warriors or cavalry together. With so much going on – Superman had arrived on the scene, too, with Dan Dare and the British Interplanetary Society, I made a decision that although the great chief would remain at the head of my hierarchy of heroes; he would become a quiet, private passion. And by then there was another radio star with his own page in the *Eagle*. PC 49 (Police Constable Archibald Berkeley-Willoughby) was an ordinary beat copper, a deft solver of crimes of all kinds. He worked for 'Q' Division of the Metropolitan Police. Played by actor Brian Reece, he filled the radio space vacated by Dick Barton, but only once a week.

The Sioux still occupied my total attention when I visited the library. I studied their hunting seasons, they way everything they needed was provided by the buffalo, and I learned how the horse had come to America with the Spaniards. All this accrued knowledge may have seemed like trivia to anyone else, but when our English teacher set us an open composition, on any subject we liked, my stories of life in the Black Hills and on the Plains always received top marks and a place on the class notice board.

My little brother, Alexander, was growing fast and in many ways his impish behaviour meant I always had to be on my guard. Often I would get home from school to discover he'd wrecked one of my space ships, and he'd done next door's cat an injury when he got hold of my catapult. Yet it would be a couple of years yet before I would have to perform that duty most big brothers have – looking after him and taking him everywhere.

In terms of misbehaviour, although I'd managed not to enrage Mam any further, and avoided more threats of boarding school, there was one occasion when I pushed Dad way over the edge and was taught an unforgettable lesson in discipline. I had added another fascination to my catalogue of obsessions – buses. There was something fascinating about EYMS single and double deckers and I often went across the road to the terminus for the Wold Road buses and, making stupid 'engine' noises, would pretend to be a bus turning around. A couple of times I had been warned by real bus drivers to stay off the road before I had an accident. The incidents had been reported to my parents by someone Mam regarded as a 'nosey neighbour', a Mrs. Wilkinson, whose whingeing little son, Bernard, I simply couldn't stand. I was warned – stay away from the buses. But I was addicted. One teatime, I decided on one more circuit of the terminus before going home to wait for Mam, who had gone with Alexander in his push-chair to the fish and chip shop for the big treat meal of the week, when Dad, on his way home, passed by on his bike. He stopped and shouted across at me. My farty, blubber-lip engine faded and I froze.

"What've you been *told*, lad! You *do not* mess around in the road near buses – now get home, smartish!"

I followed him home. Not only was this fish and chip night, it was also PC 49 night on the wireless. I was acutely apprehensive when I followed Dad into the living room. He took off his mac, then his bike clips, yet all the while facing me with a baleful stare.

"Come here!" Trembling, I stood before him and to my horror he removed his broad, ex-army Sam Brown belt.

"Bend over!"

I thought my petite derriere had been mangled by a combine harvester as the belt whacked in rapid succession across my buttocks as Dad bellowed in my ear

"When – people – tell you – to do summat – for your own – good, then you do it! If – I – catch –you – again at that bus stop (*one mighty final whack*) I'll take you to the borstal and have you kept in!"

Borstal? What new threat was this? I'd just about got over boarding school, but I knew vaguely that borstal was a place for bad lads, and as such probably even worse than Flashman. Biting my bottom lip, crying, I stood there limply hoping that he'd run out of rage. I was wrong. He picked me up bodily by the seat of my pants and the shirt collar and carried me to my bedroom. He kicked open the door and threw me in, to land heavily on the bed.

"Now stay there, damn you, until you learn to do as you're told!"

The door slammed shut. I was in a state of shock. Mam's psychological batterings were bad enough, but being flogged and thrown around by a man who had killed people in a war was an experience I did not wish to repeat.

Eventually I heard Mam return and ask Dad where I was. There were raised voices for a few moments, and I had a vague hope that Mam might have taken my side. I was now even more depressed because I could smell the fish and chips and it was almost time for PC 49 to make his appearance on the radio. Then, the door opened and suddenly Dad was towering over me.

"Right. Get up, come and get your tea and listen to the wireless."

Soon, buttocks still throbbing, I was devouring a fine fillet of battered haddock whilst my sensibilities were being soothed by another episode of Metropolitan Police life. I daren't look at Dad, but I glanced at Mam. She looked back, stern, shaking her head and going   "Tut, tut, tut ... what a bad lad ..."

Mam had got herself a job as a school cleaner, which meant she would be out every day between 4 pm and 6. Alexander went to nursery school and she would collect him on the way home, so in the time before Mam and Dad arrived home at just after six, I became a latchkey kid. Yet I didn't mind. The house was mine, and I had yet another new fascination – my friend Gilbert had been given a chemistry set for his birthday, and I'd talked him into lending it to me. I can't remember all the ingredients, but I did make some kind of 'hot ice' with baking powder and vinegar, and there was another experiment where I could produce coloured flame in a teacup. That was the experiment which landed me in a spot of bother. I burned a hole in Mam's oilcloth table cover, and cracked a teacup.

It wasn't exactly a borstal or boarding school offence, but it did result in a clip around the ear and a loss of a week's pocket money.

My cinema-going, now that I was well over nine years old, included alternative Saturdays first at the ABC Minors at Hull's city centre picture palace, the Regal, and then Saturday afternoon matinees at the Priory Cinema, which was closer to home, although when ever she was able, Mam still liked to take me to the movies on rainy afternoons. Unfortunately, my regular Saturday attendances with Gilbert, Trevor and Colin were severely marred by the sheer noisiness of the kids. It was much worse at ABC Minors, because kids from all over the city converged on the Regal for their weekly nine-penneth of film fun. The whole ABC show used to start with some song or other, which we were all expected to sing, with the lyrics on screen accompanied by a bouncing ball over the words. The tuneless racket in that cinema represented the massed, pre-pubescent wailing of an army of banshees at the gates of Hell. Once psyched up by having to sing, their lungs were permanently set at full blast, so the chances of hearing any dialogue from Flash Gordon were minimal.

Eventually, I settled for the Priory, which had better serials, and often a Lash LaRue film. Although he was a cowboy, Lash LaRue (who in real life was the more mundanely named *Alf* LaRue) was totally fascinating. He dressed completely in black, and was called Lash because of the 18 foot bullwhip he had slung over his shoulder. His adventures were well in the Hopalong Cassidy and *Lone Ranger* style, but there was a darker edge to Lash. I recently looked into what happened to him, and was saddened to see that in later life (he died in 1996) tax problems made it difficult for him to work. I was shocked to find that he'd taken the role as the villain in a porno western, *Hard on the Trail*. I haven't seen it, but the title alone stirs the imagination. But, like many misled Americans, he made up for that with a spell of repentance as a missionary for ten years. His final, crowning glory and claim to fame is that Alf LaRue was the man who taught Harrison Ford how to use a bullwhip in the *Indiana Jones* movies.

Serials were great, but even at my tender age I could see how tacky they were, with highly visible wires, wobbly, dodgy back projections, fistfights on the same old bit of scrubland every week. But there were scientific, space themes to wallow in. *Atom Man vs. Superman,* someone called Arthur Space, Brick Bradford, Buck Rogers, Flash Gordon and wicked villains of such evil genius that they made Bond's Blofeld and Goldfinger seem like social workers. Every scripted line ended with an exclamation mark with dialogue such as "Look out professor – he's got a ray gun!" And occasionally there was Ray 'Crash' Corrigan, who when he wasn't flexing his muscular torso spent the rest of his on-screen time in a gorilla suit. And of course there were robots galore, about as scientifically sophisticated as a scrap yard around the back of a boiler factory. Great, silver-painted lumbering automatons who couldn't catch a sleepy tortoise, but they scared the crap out of us. And to pounding, overwrought orchestral music, a car would plunge off a cliff at the end of each episode yet somehow, next week, the occupants had managed to survive, clinging on to that always handy tree branch, although in real life I'd never seen any trees growing out of rock cliff faces.

Some of the westerns were abysmal. I loathed and detested Roy Rogers and his ostensibly glamorous side-kick, Dale Evans. He was a 'dude' cowboy in every way – frilly shirts, embroidered boots, pearl handled revolvers, and what kind of a Wild West story is it where the villains are chased through the desert in a *jeep*? Poor old Trigger the horse was, like Dale and her unctuous beau, simply there for decoration. And then there were the inevitable treacly trail 'ballads' and 'songs' as the dude duo rode off into the fake sunset. Garbage. If Rogers was the main feature, I'd be on the bus home. Hopalong Cassidy wasn't all that much better, but at least he had the rubber-faced, rasping California Carlson as his trail mate, and Hoppy, like Lash, wore black. Needless to say, if any Indians did figure in Saturday matinees, they always stuck to the cinematic cliché of first appearing as distant, sinister silhouettes on the brow of a hill. When they attacked, it was wall to wall shrieking and whooping and usually the same bit of Monument Valley stock footage from John Ford's cutting room floor. Yet were we entertained? Damn right we were!

Over the final months at Wymersley Road, on school holidays Mam took me to as many afternoon matinees as she could. We saw them all; Humphrey Bogart, Peter Lorre, Sidney Greenstreet, Jimmy Cagney and many more. We saw 'b' movies such as *The Steel Helmet* about the Korean War, which had no stars in it of any note. Sometimes we'd see a film and be totally bamboozled or disappointed. I had never seen a full Charlie Chaplin film, and Mam always raved about how hilarious he was. So when the new Chaplin movie, *Limelight*, came out, we were first in the queue at the Royalty Cinema, armed with a quarter of lemon drops, two Mars bars and a quarter of coconut mushrooms. We left two hours later in tears. It was the saddest thing we'd ever seen, Chaplin as an elderly vaudeville act, a washed-up alcoholic clown called Calvero who helps a young dancer played by Claire Bloom. It was about as funny as a burning orphanage. Calvero dies in the wings of the theatre from a heart attack whilst his protégé is dancing on stage. Chaplin was a great artist, I'll give him that. But when I did get to see his 'tramp' movies, I simply smiled. Maybe we shouldn't have seen *Limelight* first.
We preferred Norman Wisdom.

❖ ❖ ❖ ❖

Crazy Horse and The Coalman

PART THREE:

WAY OUT WEST.

8: THE RESERVATION

"Tall and about thirty-eight years of age, he is not unlike other fine-looking and intelligent Sioux, though bearing himself with greater dignity than any of them. His eyes are exceedingly restless and impress the beholder fully as much as does his general demeanour"

Anonymous Journalist describing Crazy Horse in *The New York Sun*, May 28th 1877.

In the spring of 1877, after a winter of starvation and relentless pursuit by the U.S. Army, hell bent on revenge for Little Big Horn, Crazy Horse finally decided, against his fighting spirit and for the good of his people, to accept the Washington's offer of life on their own reservation. Many have called this a 'surrender', but as one American officer observed as Crazy Horse's dignified, 1,000 strong band approached the Indian Agency at Fort Robinson, Nebraska on May 7th,

"My God – this isn't a surrender ... it's a victory march." Feared by many, respected by his military foes, Crazy Horse, in his fierce, unremitting dignity, forced to live uncomfortably on what he called 'the white man's island' was none the less the subject of extreme jealousy among many other warriors. Thus it was that within four months his life would be over, through murder assisted by his own people. On that day when the great chief threw his people onto the Army's mercy, the U.S. Government compiled what they called a 'Surrender Ledger'. A version of this was published by the Nebraska State Historical Society in 1994. If there is any levity to be found in such a tragic scenario, it is definitely there in the names of some of the chiefs and braves listed. Try these for size; Shits On His Hand, Pisses In The Horn, Soft Prick, Snatch Stealer, Makes Widows Cry, Tanned Nuts, and the woman, Bull Proof.

Some reports list the last three names to surrender on that day as Dog Nothing, Stinking Tie and Singing Prick, although other historians believe that these last three, and an unmentioned Scabby Face, may have been given to visiting journalists as a Sioux joke – the one things the Indians always possessed was a wry sense of humour.

I enjoyed the Christmas of 1952 as much as any, with a conjuring kit, a Chad Valley six-shooter and both the *Dandy* and *Beano* annuals, yet Dad kept coming home with more news about the new houses being built in east Hull and how we'd be getting one of them. So I had this nagging feeling that the pleasure of living in the relative rural bliss of a Nissen hut on Wymersley Road would not last much longer. Each morning before school I would go out onto the golf course, dusted with a winter icing sugar of frost, and imagine all the good times I'd had there. The battles, selling golf balls, our meetings in the den. What were my parents thinking? Just because we had no bathroom, just because the roof leaked, just because Mam had to boil up a huge, coal-fired copper to do her washing, just because there was no hot and cold water – were these reasons enough to deprive me of living here?

Then in March, on a cold, rainy day, it happened. The postman brought a letter from Hull Corporation Council telling us that we had been allocated a brand new council house on Nestor Grove, off Barham Road on the Bilton Grange Estate. Mam was ecstatic. Yet oddly enough, Dad did not seem quite enthusiastic. Mam insisted that we went on the bus to Bilton Grange to look at the houses, even though it would be April before we could move in.

The whole area looked a cross between an Army manoeuvres area on Salisbury Plain and a builder's yard, but sure enough, there were the houses. We looked round one, courtesy of some building workers still applying the final touches of plastering and plumbing. There was a generous garden at the rear, and the house had two front doors; one to the entrance hall and another to a kind of utility room, upon which Dad commented

"This is just the place to keep my bike."

The main lounge was around 18ft long, with windows at each end, and the kitchen seemed to us like something in an American movie. And upstairs – there it was – a bathroom! When she saw this, Mam had tears in her eyes. A bathroom with both hot and cold water taps. I suppose I could see by Mam's response why this should represent such a domestic turning point.

So we were going to become 20th century residents in a proper house, with an immersion heater, a super lounge and somewhere to store the bike. So what, I thought. How could I be Crazy Horse in that place?

Coming here would be the equivalent of life on the reservation.

I realise today, well over half a century later, why Dad wasn't as keen as he might have been. Despite his hard life as an orphan and a professional soldier, there was a subdued, romantic side to him which I found laudable. He had *dreams*. Even as the day approached for receiving the keys to our new home, he would sit by the fire after tea reading his two favourite publications, the *Exchange & Mart* and *Farmer's Weekly*. As a mental antidote to his tough physical job as a shuttering joiner he dreamed of being a smallholder. He would often read adverts from the *Farmer's Weekly* to my puzzled Mam, such as

'Pickering, North Yorkshire. Cottage with out houses and substantial greenhouse plus 3 ½ acres of arable land'.

To which Mam would say

"Yes ... but what – why?"

Dad would sit back and draw deeply on his roll-up, looking dreamily into the middle distance.

"A few cows. Half a dozen pigs. Plant our own veg. Keep some chickens. We could have quite a life with some land in the country."

I had to admit that when I heard him wax lyrical in this manner, it also fired my imagination. Yes; we could be settlers, like in Montana or Wyoming. Maybe we'd have horses, and I could learn to ride bareback. Ever since leaving the Army after the war, Dad had been on the trail of compensation for an accident in Germany which had damaged his right arm. I have no idea how he managed to keep this legal ball in the air, but I think it was carried on by perhaps the British Legion, and just before the end of our sojourn on Wymersley Road, he had received news that a figure had been reached, probably in the region of around £1,000, which was quite a sum in 1953. It would still, however, be a few months before this case would be finalised, but it was fuel to his roaring dreams. No doubt this was his only chance in life, as a wage-earning working man, to follow those dreams. The problem was, we'd be dragged along with them.

One day we had a visit from my sea-going Uncle Laurie, and his wife, Auntie Flo. For some health reason she remained childless. Flo was a spritely little woman who spent 70% of her time alone, with Laurie mostly at sea on the Hull-Denmark run. She was unafraid to express her sometimes unwelcome opinions on the comings and goings of our branch of the family, but was often wise enough to do so out of Dad's earshot. I was intrigued on this particular visit when she leant towards Mam, who had outlined Dad's agricultural obsessions, in a conspiratorial fashion,

"That's the trouble with Stan. He's a gunner."

I wondered what this military designation had to do with his pioneering spirit.

"How do you mean?" asked Mam.

"Well," said Flo, grinning, "he's always gunner do this and gunner do that, yet he always does nothing."

We moved house on a very wet Monday in May. On the Saturday I had a final meeting of my 'gang' in the den in the hedge. It was a sad affair. I'd be losing Barbara, and although Gilbert, Colin and Trevor said we ought to keep in touch, in our little universe Bilton Grange might as well have been the dark side of the moon. No, I would simply have to start all over again. That Monday seemed like my surrender to the white man. We all sat in the back of the removal van once we'd loaded up and I cried as I saw our hut and the golf course recede into the rainy distance. Life would never be the same again.

Once on the new estate, we experienced a very odd, major cock-up when the removal van had left. Exhausted from all the fetching and carrying, we were slumped on our tatty old settee catching our breath, our wet clothes steaming. It was then that we discovered the house we had moved into was the wrong one. Apparently there had been a mix-up with the keys. At three in the afternoon, just as we were making a cup of tea, another family arrived on our doorstep. Somehow, we had got their keys and house number, but the documentation they held showed without doubt that this was their address, they had brought our keys, and ours was further along the block, about four houses away. In torrential rain we moved every bit of furniture, every box and stuffed tea chest along the street, accompanied by little Alexander's persistent wailing.

It was strange spending that first night in a new bedroom which smelled of fresh plaster and wood shavings. And there was a curious rumble every few minutes, which Dad explained was the mysterious immersion heater, a cylindrical copper tank full of hot water. I asked Mam what would happen if the water kept boiling and rumbling and she inadvertently put the fear of God into me.

"Well – I suppose if it's left switched on and the water keeps boiling and we don't run any off, then the tank could explode."

Oh, *terrific* – and it was in a cupboard next to my headboard! Life was much simpler at Wymersley Road.

I got up the following day and the rain had gone, so I went out onto the massive building site to see what adventures I might have. As I lurked around in a pile of timber roof trusses, I suddenly came face to face with a bespectacled boy of about my age wearing the complete regalia of a Cub Scout.

"Who are you?" he asked, looking me up and down.

"I'm called Roy. We moved into Nestor Grove yesterday." I was intrigued by his rig.

"Is this a scouting place?" I asked.

"No. I just like wearing these things. Like a uniform. Makes me look special. A bit tough."

I disagreed, but didn't say anything. Tough? Wait until I tell you about Crazy Horse, I thought. Then you'll know what tough is. I knew about the Cubs and the Scouts but I'd never thought about joining them.

"What do cubs do, then?"

"I'm a Wolf Cub. We help people, do jobs, play games in the church hall with Arkela. She's our leader. And we go camping in the countryside."

This last bit appealed to me.

"What's your name?" I asked.

"Barry Thompson. I go to Bilton Grange School. That's where I should be today but I'm off poorly. My Mam doesn't know I'm out. She thinks I'm in bed."

I knew there was something in the Cubs about being honest and true, so this Barry seemed to be letting the side down. Naturally, our family weren't settled in enough yet to pack me off to a new school, something I was dreading. I left Barry to continue his lurk among the trusses with the promise that I'd meet him at school the following week. I began to wonder about being a Wolf Cub. That bit about camping in the country appealed to me. I made a note to tell Mam and Dad.

The following Monday Dad was back at work, and Mam, pushing Alexander in his push chair, accompanied me to my new school. In many ways it was similar to Wold Road.

Probably built in the late 1930s, with a large assembly hall and a pupil clientele of roughly the same social mix; the slightly better heeled and the raggedy arses like myself. My teacher was to be a Mr. Pickford, and he seemed a pleasant sort. That said, when consumed by mathematics, he turned into the usual academic demon capable of inflicting ridicule on numerical dunces such as me. I got to meet Barry Thompson again and we became great friends, because when I began outlining my obsession with Crazy Horse he remained attentive and fascinated. Yet I knew there would be no more battle re-enactments, because somehow I felt as if I was growing out of that area. I was reading more, drawing and looking forward to each English lesson.

Towards the end of May 1953 we were all told about the forthcoming coronation of the new Queen, and that we would be receiving a coronation mug and spoon. Even better – we'd be having a day off from school.

The day of the coronation, June 2nd, was wet and blustery. Mam made a special dinner of battered coley, chips, and a huge pan of mushy peas. We accompanied this with freshly baked bread baked in our sparkling new gas oven. At night there was to be a firework display, and in a large hall nearby they were going to show free films to anyone interested. During the day, the coronation had been broadcast on the new fangled BBC television service. Barry Thompson said he had a mate whose parents had a TV set, so I met him shortly after dinner to make our way to his mate's house on Barham Road. It was by then raining heavily, and when we got to the house, we faced quite a disappointment. Barry knocked on the door and his friend, Eric, answered it.

"What do you want?"

"Er... can we watch the coronation on your television?" asked Barry.

"I'll have to ask my Mam," said Eric. A few seconds later, Eric's mother appeared, a prim little woman in a pink dress and horn-rimmed glasses. She looked us up and down.

"Who are you two then?"

"I'm Eric's mate from school," said Barry, "and this is Roy. He's just moved in around the corner."

She gave us the kind of look one might give a vagrant who had defecated on your doorstep.

"Well, I don't know you and you're both absolutely wet through, so you'd make a mess on my furniture. If you want to watch the coronation you can, but you'll have to stand in the front garden and watch it through the window." At that the door slammed in our faces.

And so it came to pass that two rain-soaked ten year olds stood in a muddy bed of geraniums, their noses pressed against wet glass, straining to see a flickering 9 inch screen at the opposite end of Eric's lounge. What made it worse was that they were all drinking lemonade and eating cake. I think this was my ultimate Tiny Tim moment. All we could see were vague, ghostly images of somebody in a big white frock surrounded by lofty blokes in frock coats and garters. After twenty minutes of this punishment, Barry and I headed back to our respective homes, and I spent the rest of the afternoon reading my new *Big Book of Space Travel*.

Mam told me that we'd be going to the hall that night for the free films, which included an interesting western called *The Dalton Gang* starring someone with the fruity name of 'Red' Berry.

As there were quite a lot of mushy peas left from dinner Mam had been out and bought a ham shank, and with the meat from this and some onions, had created a large pan of pea and ham soup for our tea, accompanied by more fresh bread. This was turning out to be quite a gourmet day.

Dad didn't want to come with us to see *The Dalton Gang*, so volunteered to stay home with Alexander, thus allowing Mam and I, the real cineastes, to set off for a genuine treat – free films, no doubt courtesy of the monarchy.

The hall, I think it was a church hall, was packed, and the

vicar was operating the projector. There were rows of tubular steel and canvas chairs, and we managed to get seats about four rows from the front. The sound was good, the screen, although smaller of course than a cinema's, was adequate, and the night started well with three *Looney Tunes* cartoons, which had us all in stitches. We were only about 30 minutes into *The Dalton Gang* when I became aware of a foul stench creeping across our row. It abated, and then minutes later returned with a vengeance. It had a sulphurous, eggy thrust to it and seemed to enter one's nostrils accompanied by an insistent heat. This being a day of national celebration, there were two drunks in the row behind us, one of whom I heard say

"Bloody *hell,* Harry – has summat crawled up your arse and *died?"* To which Harry responded

"No, but I'm puttin' this ciggie out – if we keep smokin' this hall could go up."

Then three ladies in front of us turned and scanned along our row, tut-tutting and waving their delicate hankies in front of their noses. In the flickering light from the screen, I could see Mam looking annoyed. Suddenly, she grabbed me by the arm.

"Come on, I can't be doing with this. Let's go home. They wouldn't put up with this in the Regal or the Londesborough."

So, sadly I never got to see *The Dalton Gang* in its entirety. Come to think of it, I still haven't seen it.

Back home Alexander was in bed asleep and Dad was drinking a bottle of beer and listening to Henry Hall on the wireless. Mam made us both a cup of cocoa and by 9.30, I was in bed. As she tucked me in, Mam seemed a little quiet and withdrawn.

"Shame we had to come home early, Mam."

"Never mind son, I'll make it up to you." She gave me a kiss and as she moved towards the bedroom door I heard a slight creaky, squeaky noise. The door closed. Suddenly, I was overcome with the Dalton Gang's sulphurous odour again. I thrust my head under the blankets.

Two meals in one day featuring mushy peas – and the dangerous addition of onions – can have devastating results.

As 1953 rolled on I was still homesick for Wymersley Road. I had a few new friends, but they were no match for Gilbert and Barbara. I was doing well in English at school and Mr. Pickford always praised my written compositions and pinned them on the class notice board. One in particular, entitled *Havoc*, he actually read aloud to the class. It involved an alien race who were orbiting the earth and controlling our weather, causing meteorological devastation.

At Christmas I got the part of Scrooge in the school play, a heavily edited and truncated version of *A Christmas Carol*.
But it wasn't a good Christmas. Dad was still going on about his smallholding dream whilst Mam was trying to settle into our new life. Every night he would find some new advert in the *Exchange & Mart* or *Farmer's Weekly* to read out aloud, and he chipped away at Mam's resolve to stay put. In December Dad lost his job again and as Christmas loomed we were broke. Christmas dinner that year was two rabbits in a stew with roast potatoes, and a Christmas pudding held over from the previous year. We were, as usual, in debt to the coal man, but at least our supply lasted out until New Year's Eve.

One day in March 1954, just before my eleventh birthday, Dad came home one night and was over the moon when he opened a letter from the Government containing his cheque from his 1945 accident.
Mam had discovered she was pregnant again. This gave her various mood swings and as he continued his campaign to move to the country, especially now that he had some capital, she finally cracked and became interested in the idea.
The Baintons were about to go west.

❖ ❖ ❖ ❖

9: PAHA SAPA

*'It does not matter where his body lies,
for it is grass; but where his spirit is, it will be good to be'*

Black Elk on the Killing of Crazy Horse.

Dad's plans took shape rapidly. I think Mam, being pregnant, had given up the fight for us to stay put in our new home. Dad had already, through the column headed 'Smallholdings' in the *Exchange & Mart*, picked out his dream 'ranch' high on a hill in the Calder Valley above the Yorkshire town of Mytholmroyd, which sits between Halifax and Hebden Bridge. He'd been to a phone box, spoken to the farmer who owned the property, who had sent us information and some photographs in the post. The financial details were sketchy. I have no idea what kind of deal was involved, but it meant Dad parting with most of his army compensation, with just a little left over for moving house and buying his much-desired livestock.

Photographs, especially indistinct black and white Brownie 'snaps' as they were in those days, can be deceptive. Oh, and how. Yet there was this block of compact-looking stone cottages on a hillside surrounded by fields, and in the distance, something we never saw around Hull – hills. Big hills; tall, sloping to the sky hills. To me they became the Sioux's beloved Paha Sapa – my own Black Hills. This looked like it might be fun, after all, although the prospect of starting at yet another school was not welcome.

The amazing thing about this chapter in our lives was that Dad would make all the decisions as to the domestic suitability of his chosen smallholding – and those decisions were made arbitrarily by him on a solo day's visit to Mytholmroyd. So, Mam and we three boys were about to leave our new house for a location we had never seen, many miles from our native turf. There were no interior photos of the house, but Dad's glowing sales job when he arrived back at 10pm from his trip would have made an estate agent proud.

"Oh, the fresh air! Birds singing, rolling fields, heather on the moors. It's a solid old house, built to last, and there's some out buildings. I spoke to the farmer about getting a couple of cows and he'll sell us some pigs and chickens."

I could see Mam softening to this. It sounded like heaven.

Then he turned to me.

"It'll be like the wild west, lad! You'll have all the space in the world – you'll be like a real Indian!"

It was planned for us to move in July, by which time poor Mam would be 8 months pregnant.

In the run-up to this new development, before anything had been finalised, I had accepted Barry Thompson's invitation to go to the church hall on Cubs night to see if I could join 'the pack'. To be honest, I didn't think much to the junior clan of the knobbly knees and the woggle. Nor, I could tell, did they think much to this little scruff in their midst. But I was made welcome by Arkela, an earnest young pony-tailed woman in full regalia and heavy horn rims. But the games we played seemed stupid. Something to do with being chased by a wolf, then a session tying knots, then some rather dumb songs. There was a lot of running up and down and shouting, but Little Big Horn this wasn't. It would be pointless trying to get this regimented gaggle of mini Baden-Powells into a Sioux frame of mind. I gave my name and address and Arkela told me that as soon as there was a vacancy in the pack – a vacancy? (What was this – the Freemasons?) then she would let me know.

I heard nothing else. In fact, I'm still waiting.

However, with Barry, there were other games we played. One day, out with Mam in Hull we bought a bag of 'assorted clothing' from a junk shop.

When we got home, among the moth-eaten shirts and washed-out dungarees were two flags – one merchant navy Red Duster and the flag of South Africa. The South African flag was a vivid orange, white and blue, and it was about 2 feet by 4. I decided that it would make an

excellent super-hero cloak. I could never decide which superhero to be, and Barry had already purloined the role of Batman because his Mam had given him some black cloth for a cloak, and sewn some 'ears' onto his balaclava. So, with my blue swimming trunks over my pants and my South African cloak, I became 'Captain Mystery'. We did stupid things like jumping off piles of bricks and timber, and pretending to fight, but it wasn't Crazy Horse.

Sadly, I had just begun to get used to my new life on Bilton Grange when it was time to leave. Even Major, our dog, seemed nervous, and our budgie, Tommy, had been quiet all day. The night before we made the crucial move, Mam and Dad organised a special treat. It took two bus rides but it was worth it. We all went to the West Park Cinema to see Laurel and Hardy in *Way Out West*. I suppose it had some resonance to what was to come. It was the last laugh we'd have for a while.

On that fateful July morning a large removal van arrived, and Dad helped the 2-man crew to load up. When I went to carry the budgie cage, to my horror, I looked into it and there was Tommy, lying in a pile of millet seeds, stiff and dead. It seemed like some kind of omen as we wrapped him in newspaper and buried him in the garden.

We didn't have much; our beds, a wardrobe, dressing table, a couple of rugs, kitchen cabinet, a ragged three piece suite and a table and chairs. I noticed that we loaded our all-important Stella radio, and hoped we would be set up in the Black Hills in time for the new radio serial, *Journey into Space*. One thing

Dad had failed to mention was that, yet again, we were plunging back into medieval existence with no electricity, no gas, and no running water. But those sad facts were still to be discovered. Once the van was fully loaded, Dad lifted Mam onto the tailboard and the rest of us followed. This was a real adventure, because they had placed our three piece suite facing out of the back of the van so that we could travel with our furniture and, with the top half of the rear van doors left open, whilst not being able to see where we were going, we could at least see where we'd been.

By now Mam had entered into Dad's spirit of occasion.

"It's just like being on a wagon train," she enthused, beaming, "we're going way out west for a new life!" She had made two flasks of tea, packed a large bottle of lemonade, some sandwiches, potato crisps, Mars bars and pork pies. Dad locked up the house, presented the keys to a man from the council, and as I sat there on our settee looking over the tailgate a sudden wave of sadness and foreboding overcame me. I looked at that fine, solid house, and realised that, in many ways, I had, without realising it, begun to be happy there. But now it was empty, locked, and as Dad clambered alongside us the removal van belched into life and we began to pull away. Seeing our home recede into the distance almost made me cry, but a Fletcher's pork pie was always an all-round palliative. The journey took almost three hours, with two toilet stops. Just after three o'clock in the afternoon we rolled into the Calder Valley, which was just suffering the tail-end of a rainstorm, and Dad was in his element, pointing out landmarks, fields and farms. Exciting though it was, it still seemed an alien landscape to me, and Alexander was crying, saying he wanted to go home.

"We're *going* home, son," said Dad, "to our new house!"

We entered Mytholmroyd and the first thing we noticed was the steepness of the hills rising from each side of the town, through which ran the River Calder. The van coughed, rumbled and strained, going up a hill at a somewhat precarious angle, then through some woodland over a bumpy track, eventually coming to a halt outside a farm house. A stout, red-faced man in wellingtons, a flat cap and a duffel coat appeared, and waved a knobbly walking stick at us.

"Here he is," said Dad, as if this character was a long lost friend. "That's our man – farmer Brown."

The florid farmer stood at the rear of the van, looking disdainfully at this quintet of tired faces. He didn't smile. I think he'd seen too many gypsies before. He walked around the van and met the driver who was climbing out of the cab.

"Now then. As y'can see, lad, the road ends here – just a cow track, and it's muddy. Reckon if y'take this big wagon on any further tha'll get stuck – and I ain't turning t'tractor out t'pull yer out."

Mam listened to this and looked at me.

"He sounds helpful, I'm sure. Miserable sod."

From the snapshots we could recognise the cottage, a good 800 yards away across the field, but it seemed obvious there was no proper road to it. This was as rustic as it got.

There were no words of welcome. It was getting late in the afternoon and we could all have done with a cup of tea.

The fact that we had travelled, two small kids with a heavily pregnant mother, all this way in a furniture van, seemed to mean nothing to this sour-faced son of the soil. He looked over the tailgate at our scruffy furniture.

"Well, tha'll 'ave t'git this lot carried across t'field if tha wants t'get t'bed toneet! No good sittin' up there, eh?"

Dad and I eventually managed to put an easy chair down on the grass so that Mam had somewhere to rest. For the next ninety minutes, what transpired was like something from a 'Big White Hunter' yarn or Tales of The Raj, as the two removal men and Dad struggled along the muddy track towards the sombre looking cottage carrying items of furniture, with me following on with anything I could reasonably lift.

When I reached the front door of our new home, Dad turned the key in the weather-beaten old oak door and I was staggered.

This was far worse than a sod cabin in outer Montana. I tried to rustle up some pioneering spirit but it wasn't there. I looked back across the field to where Mam was sitting in her chair. She looked tired, yet I knew that once she'd come face to face with Dad's 'dream' home she'd have more than exhaustion to contend with.

The house was a low affair, faced by a stone-built bank which supported the field above. This flag-stoned gully in front of the ground floor windows, where stood a hand-cranked water pump, made the house dark and dismal. The walls were three feet thick, the windows tiny. Inside the stone floors felt damp and cold. The kitchen area, such as it was, looked out onto the stone-clad bank. There was a large earthenware sink and scrubbed pine draining board. Everything seemed cramped and oppressive and I could not help contrasting it to the bright, modern home we had left behind in Hull only hours before. The second room on this ground floor had the same tiny windows and a large fireplace. It looked out on the fields rolling down to the town of Mytholmroyd below. The two bedrooms were more depressing; they seemed darker still, smelled fusty, and even though it was July I could tell that winter in this place was
going to make our life in a Nissen hut seem like a suite at the Ritz. Yet, as he helped the two removal men, smiling, joking and puffing on his cigarette, it seemed obvious to me that Dad was in some kind of pioneer heaven. Then, after a muddy struggle across the field, Mam arrived at the front door. He looked at her, beaming, awaiting her rapture. He was out of luck. She scanned the façade of the building then stepped inside. There were tears in her eyes. She sighed heavily.

"Oh ... my good God ... what have you done ... what *have* you done?" Dad stoically kept on beaming.

"Not bad, is it?" Mam looked at him and gasped.

"Not bloody bad? *Not bad?* Look at it! It's like the tower of bloody London! There's no water, no gas, no light switches, no lights, it'll be like living in a cave! How am I going to bring a child into the world in this dump?"
Dad's smile faded and he left the house and went to settle up with the removal men. I heard the van go, and it seemed that our umbilical cord with the real world had finally been severed. Mam sat down heavily on a dining chair by the window and stared out at the town below, her eyes still filled with tears. She gestured to me to go to her. I did and she put an arm around my shoulder.

"What do you think, son?"

"I think what you think, Mam," I replied. "It's not very nice. It feels like a sad place. I wish we weren't here."

For that first two weeks at Mytholmroyd, Dad was about as popular as a porcupine in a balloon factory. Mam worked in silence day by day trying to make the house feel like home. However, there were two cottages in this block and Dad had never warned us that we had neighbours. On our first morning there, the couple next door, Dennis and his wife Lily, made themselves known to us in the company of their 8 year old daughter, Susan. They brought us half a dozen new-laid eggs and I think this went some way into lifting Mam's depression.

But there was something about this family I didn't like. Dennis was a dark-eyed, brown haired bloke in his late 30s, with an eternal smirk on his face. Lily was a thin, anaemic looking woman, slightly older than her husband, her black hair streaked with grey. She didn't smile much, and there was something in her wide, round darting eyes which made me think she was frightened of something or other. As for Susan, blue-eyed, pigtailed, standing there in her pink cotton dress and grey cardigan, she seemed to direct most of her unsmiling gaze towards the floor. Mam was still mastering the iron fittings on the fireplace with the huge cast-iron kettle, and had managed to make a pot of tea. Dennis did most of the talking,

telling Dad where he could buy some pigs, and offering him the chance to go halves with his flock of 70 laying hens, for a small investment. Needless to say, Dad went for the deal.
But when the family left, Mam simply said;
"I don't like them – and he's a bit creepy..." I had to agree.

It had been fortunate that we had moved early during our school holidays and with several weeks still remaining before facing the horror of yet another new school I would at least have the opportunity to explore the new landscape. I had to admit, in some ways, up on the high moors away from civilisation, the territory did give me an inkling of what Crazy Horse's beloved Paha Sapa, the Black Hills, might be like. Armed with my trusty catapult and a newly-made bow and arrows, I wandered about a mile away from home on day and came upon a dramatic outcrop of rocks where some boys were already playing. They were about my age, and at first regarded me with some suspicion. The largest, a rough looking lad with a shock of ginger hair, confronted me and looked at my catapult and bow and arrows. He asked who I was and where I lived. I told him. He pointed to the rocks.
"These is our rocks 'ere. We call'em Robin 'ood's rocks. I'm Will Scarlet and we're the merry men. D'yer wanna join our gang?" I could see no point in refusing. Over the next hour, using my bow and catapult to knock tin cans off the tallest rock, I managed to acquit myself fairly well. Then we all sat down for a while on a big, flat rock and I brought up the subject of Crazy Horse. The argument went that they didn't think he was as good as Robin Hood, but when I told them about his battles and the size of his forces, they seemed suitably impressed. I went home that night feeling slightly better.

One thing Dad did do in those early Mytholmroyd days was something I had always wished for when we lived on Wymersley Road. Utilising some old pram wheels and two large, sturdy wooden orange boxes, he made us a bogie. I suppose today you'd call it a powerless go-kart, the kind of thing you'd enter into a soapbox derby. Yet ours was larger than many of the ones owned by my mates, which I'd seen back in Hull. Both Alexander and I could get into it and there would still be plenty of room.

However, Dad had an ulterior motive. One day in the first week of August he told me to put my wellingtons on and accompany him on a journey, pulling the bogie on a length of rope, across some very basic moorland tracks. Eventually we arrived at a remote farm, from which emanated a lot of squealing and grunting and foul smell.

Soon, after a transaction with yet another dour, taciturn ruddy-faced local farmer, involving the presentation of large, white Bank of England five pound notes, the two boxes on the bogie each contained three pink squealing piglets.

Back home we housed the noisy piglets in the wooden out house in the field. Dad was in his element again. Sitting around the table in the grim candlelight that night eating Irish stew, he proclaimed

"Well, we're getting there, eh? Chickens and eggs, that's done, now we've got the pigs – they'll grow up and make money. Maybe we'll look for a milk cow now. What d'you think?"

Mam yawned and held her distended belly.

"And now we not only have to feed ourselves, but six pigs for God knows how long. Heaven knows what good a cow's going to be."

There was much we sorely missed over those early nights. Our comics. Friends. The soothing background of the radio, for example; now all we heard was the clock ticking. I hated the candles and the oil lamps, and the pokey fireplace which belched smoke back into the room at every puff of wind outside. I would lie in bed in the pitch blackness thinking "How long can this go on?"

On Saturday August 7th the sun was out and it was warm, but Mam was feeling unwell, and seemed to be in pain. By 12 noon she went to bed and Dad had gone to Farmer Brown's house and asked to use the phone. When he returned, he gave me a ten shilling note.

"Is there a picture house in Mytholmroyd?" he asked.

"No," I said, "Susan next door says there's only one in Hebden Bridge and you have to get the bus."

He looked concerned as I stood there with the money, wondering what all this was about.

"Now, your Mam, upstairs in bed, is having a baby. I want you to go into town, take Alexander, get the bus to Hebden Bridge and go to the pictures. You can keep the change. If there isn't a Saturday matinee, come straight home. You'll have a surprise waiting for you."

Alexander had just turned six years old and facing this unknown journey in a strange environment whilst looking after him seemed a great responsibility, but I could see a touch of desperation in Dad's face.

The afternoon went well. It was only a twenty minute bus ride, and the superb Hebden Bridge Picture House did have a kid's matinee – with no less than an Atom Man serial and a Lash LaRue movie! This, plus the fact we could afford ice creams and a packet of crisps, turned our mission into quite an adventure.

When we arrived back at the cottage, as we walked along the flagstones outside, we could hear a baby crying. As we entered, we met the District Midwife who was cleaning some utensils in the kitchen sink. She smiled at us. Dad appeared, and seemed relieved to see us.

"Aha! Now then, be very quiet and gentle, go upstairs to Mam and Dad's bedroom – and meet your new brother."

And there he was; a pink, chubby-faced bundle of joy wrapped in a crocheted white shawl. I was taken aback at how washed out poor Mam looked. She had bruises on her hands, and her eyes were red, her face pale. But I could see that underneath it all, she was happy. Alexander took one of the baby's tiny hands and I took hold of the other.

"Has he got a name?" I asked.

"Yes," said Mam, "he's going to be called Patrick Stanley."

As the weeks progressed Alexander and I were taken to our new school, and I could tell from the start that we weren't going to be popular. There was a project going at the school based around Edmund Hilary's conquest of Everest earlier in the year. We had samples of the foodstuffs the mountaineers had enjoyed on their ascent, and in my class we were asked to write a composition about what it was like to be a mountain climber. I did my best, but the unfamiliar surroundings and general domestic depression did not bode well for sparkling prose.

In the dense woodland further down the valley slopes there was another rock face. I met Will Scarlet (I never did know his real name) regularly and he told me that earlier in the year the whole town of Mytholmroyd had been flooded, and that he had secretly saved some boxes of stuff which had floated down the street from a chemist's shop. One day he decided he would show me his hoard, which was hidden in a crevice in the rock face, a kind of cave with a dead end. There were several large, stained cardboard cartons. They contained thousands of Dr. Scholl's corn plasters, bunion cushions and heel plasters. Why the hell Will would think these had any value was beyond me. However, I took some samples home and Mam, who suffered with bunions, was highly pleased. At first they thought I'd robbed a chemist's or attacked a chiropodist with my catapult, but when I explained the illicit booty's origins, Dad seemed relaxed about it all. He even asked if I could get hold of more, and after several trips to the cave we soon had a cupboard full of enough foot care to last a decade.

Nights were restless with new-born Patrick crying,

Alexander tossing and turning in bed worried about school, which he hated. And I could hardly sleep because I was due to leave the juniors and attend the middle school in Hebden Bridge. This would part me and my little brother and neither of us was looking forward to it.

The school in Hebden Bridge seemed awful. It had a very rural middle-class, snobbish atmosphere and, dressed as I was in cut-down 8th Army Desert Rat shorts, Royal Navy pullovers and truncated wellingtons which looked like galoshes, I provided the bullies and wags in my class – and others – with all the excuses they needed to practice their dark art of ridicule. My only relief came from two lessons – music, where we actually listened to gramophone records, and something new to me – domestic science. I chose the latter from a trio of options, which included metalwork and woodwork. Realising I'd be lousy at both, I opted for cookery lessons with the girls.

And then we got a new form teacher called Miss Carroll, and I fell in love. She was slim, bespectacled, and blonde and perhaps around 25, and she defended me against the bullies, and took an interest in my work. Whenever I could, I would leave a flower on her desk, sometimes, if I could afford it, an apple. We were passing through a period where the steel-nibbed pen and the school inkwell were about to be slowly replaced by the biro. I didn't have a biro pen, but Miss Carroll brought one to school for me, and presented me with it one afternoon when the class was emptying after an English lesson. As I felt her soft hand touch mine as she gave me the pen, my heart raced.

"Now you can write some more of your nice compositions about the Sioux Indians," she said, gently. I wanted to kiss her.

As the months rolled on and Christmas loomed, all was not going well for Dad and his smallholding dream. He had naively imagined that, if he had some pigs and chickens, and somewhere to live, then that would be all he needed to run the home. But now his remaining army money had expired, and the arrangement he had with the unpleasant farmer Brown, which, I believe, included a deposit on the house and a private agreement to pay so much per month, had fallen into arrears. Weekly Brown would arrive on the doorstep and make loud threats about eviction. With only a narrow lane, impassable to large vehicles, leading up to our house, we had to use the bogie to go to the coal merchants in town for our fuel. It was a weekly trial which both I and my Dad dreaded. The rest of the time Dad cut green wood from the forest, an act which frequently got him into trouble, but it was slow to burn.

Christmas, cold, grim and dark, was made bearable only by the fact that we had Patrick, our new family member, to celebrate with us. He was a sweet yet noisy baby, and we all loved him. We got some comics, a Beano annual and some jigsaws that year, but at least we had a roast chicken, which was a genuine delicacy, brought to the candle-lit table with great pride and ceremony. Yet if only we'd had a radio. I missed all the joys of Luxembourg and Dan Dare, and PC 49. Our house was often as silent as a tomb.

At the end of January farmer Brown gave us a month's notice to quit. Dad, his rural dream over, had no choice other than to sell the pigs, which by now had grown considerably, and the chickens. We had no longer had any money to feed these animals. It seemed pointless to waste the money raised from the sales on staying in that awful house. So Dad decided to find work once again as a joiner, and was taken on by a building firm in Hebden Bridge. With less than three weeks left before we were expected to vacate the house, he pulled off a master stroke. His firm had been doing some work on a new barn for a farmer at the other side of the valley, and Dad noticed that the farm had two tied cottages nearby, both empty. He met with the farmer, made some kind of deal, and within a month, with great difficulty, we had moved from one medieval hovel to another medieval hovel. I thought that things couldn't get worse – yet by staying the same, they did.

The house we moved to had a kind of Hound of The Baskervilles feel to it. It had tall, leaded rectory windows and in the dark, windowless entrance hall, above the kitchen door, hung the stuffed head of a deer. The effect of seeing this wall-mounted decapitation every night was similar to the sinister paranoia engendered by the Laughing Cavalier back in Queen's Terrace. We did have an extra bedroom, though, and a larger kitchen, and this house had the luxury of a standing water tap in the kitchen. But once again, no electricity and no gas. But there was something else; a large timber shed which Dad would use for a workshop, and a ramshackle greenhouse, which he soon repaired. And then, with his new wages, Dad did something to bring a little ray of joy back into our lives.

One Saturday, he went into town to the electrical shop and bought a second hand *Ever Ready* Model C portable radio. I know it must have cost at least £5 and the huge chunky batteries were not cheap. His outlay that day must have represented most of a week's wages, but the pleasure it brought us was sublime. He had also improved the lighting in our rotten old Transylvanian castle. He'd bought three Tilley lamps, brass beauties called 'storm lanterns' which, after ignition with methylated spirits, ran on paraffin. They had a gas mantle, and the paraffin was delivered under pressure, so that the lamp had to be pumped up every night before use, and if the light began to fade, more instant pumping was required. Yet the light they gave was as close to electricity or piped gas, as we could possibly get. At least we didn't suffer from eye-strain when reading our comics, and the radio ... *oh, the radio!* Although we had to conserve the expensive batteries by only allowing a couple of hours of broadcasting every night, at least we were once again tuned into the goings-on on the greater planet earth.

Living at the other side of Mytholmroyd, despite the few domestic improvements, was just as bad as it could be. Little Patrick was growing, but not in the kind of environment a modern baby deserved.

My trips to school at Hebden Bridge were now longer than ever. The house was high up on the hill and it took a 30 minute walk through wild moorland to get to the bus stop. If, for any reason, I missed the bus back from school, it meant a five mile walk with a steep climb and a trudge along dark, sinister lanes flanked by tall dry stone walls.

My social position at school was still one of ridicule. I knew that by now, aged 11, I ought to be on the verge of having some long trousers, but to my dismay my new autumn term outfit was as outlandish as ever. Alexander had to wear similar garb; our ex-army shorts seemed to have got bigger, with legs which stuck out like inverted power station cooling towers. We also had some new Royal Navy sailor's shirts with square necklines, complete with blue piping. Our khaki socks were made for men, so they became slack after a minute's walking, and could only be held up with fierce, circulation-strangling elastic garters. The snobbery of my classmates seemed to cross a new border – it began to affect the teachers, with the laudable exception of the delicious Miss Carroll.

One day, in the school dinner hall, I was about to begin eating my meat and potato pie when I became aware of our arithmetic teacher, Mr. Lister, hovering at my shoulder. My fork stopped in mid-air as he began his embarrassing outburst.

"Now then, children. Take a look here – this is how the little piggies eat down on the farm." The long table exploded with laughter. But he wasn't finished.

"If you listen carefully, he'll make some piggy noises – and he doesn't even know how to use his cutlery."

I felt sick, angry and on the verge of tears, but I ate my dinner because I was hungry.

That night, the incident haunted me, and Mam, always perceptive when it came to her kids, put an arm around me.

"What's the matter, son?"

I told her about Lister's comments in detail. She patted me on the hands and said "Don't you worry. God'll deal with him."

The next day, in the dining hall, I was dreading another embarrassing interruption, but this time everyone got more than they bargained for. Lister was standing at the head of the table, glancing from child to child, looking ready to launch into more sarcasm, when suddenly, the double doors to the dining hall burst noisily open. There, framed in the doorway, stood my Mam, her headscarf tight on her head, her shopping bag at her side. She was pushing a Tansad (a 1950s version of a baby buggy) containing a heavily swaddled little Patrick. She was a short and stocky woman – and I'll agree, like the rest of us (apart from Dad) bordering on the obese. But she looked nothing like my mother that day. She looked like an avenging angel; angry, steely-eyed. She strode across the hall floor pushing the Tansad, and came face to face with Lister.

"Are you Mr Lister?"

"Yes, madam – can I help you?"

"No – but you can help yourself. This lad here –"
she gestured to me, "is my son. I bring him up the best way I can. So get this – if I hear that you've called him a 'little piggie' ever again, I'll swing for you – you're a bloody disgrace. And I'll see the headmaster, and report you to the education board. Now keep your snobby ideas to yourself and let the kids alone!"

The blood had drained from Lister's face. I could see him trying to form some kind of response, but Mam had turned on her heel, and with Tansad wheels squeaking, sailed out through the hall doors. I had no more trouble after that. Looking back, I realise the sheer effort she had made that day, struggling across country to the bus stop, pushing that little pram, as she seethed with anger. God bless her.

There were no shops up on the hill where we lived, but there was a rather curious source of supply for various comestibles, tinned stuff, lard, sugar etc. In my class at school there was only one boy who seemed to match my domestic poverty. He had the grand name of Hector McCready. His mother lived about a mile from our house along a remote lane which cut across the moors. Rather than trek down the hill into

Mytholmroyd for odd items, it was sometimes necessary to visit Mrs. McCready's bedroom store.

One dark October night I had to walk home from school, by choice, because Mam wished me to cut across the moorland to pick up some sugar and baked beans. Hector walked with me. It was dark and rainy, and our legs were wet and cold. When we reached Hector's house, I could see the oil lamps burning in the bedroom window, which was on the ground floor.

Mrs. McCready was a portly woman of indeterminate age. She had wild, red hair, streaked with silver, rotting teeth and the kind of eyes Bela Lugosi would have died for. We never firmly established what incapacitating illness she suffered from, but it may well have been advanced lung cancer. Because of this, she lived her whole life propped up in a single bed in a small, nicotine-stained room. All around her, above the headboard and on the nearby walls, were cupboards, all within arm's reach. In these she kept her 'goods' as she called them. These were replenished every two weeks from shops in Hebden Bridge by Mr. McCready, who had a bicycle and trailer. Standing there with one's brown paper carrier bag, you would read out your order, and like a flailing windmill Mrs. McCready would prod open the relevant cupboard doors and toss the required goods onto her bedding. Yet there was one aspect to shopping McCready style which would have provided current Health and Safety Environment Jobsworths with a combination of cardiac arrest and severe legal work.

On the bedside table, with its oil lamp and overflowing ashtray full of Capstan Full Strength dog ends stood a large pickle jar. At the end of every sentence Mrs. McCready spoke, she would reach for the jar, and deposit a thick stream of glutinous green mucus into it, adding to the pint of gloop already visible. I often wondered whose job it was to empty that foul receptacle. She wasn't an unpleasant lady, in fact she was kind, despite the fact that locals referred to her as 'the Witch'. In her misfortune, she just wasn't all that hygienic.

As October grew darker and colder, a terrible event occurred which would alter our immediate lives for the worse.
I don't know what it is with agricultural types, but the farmers we always dealt with were trouble. Perhaps it's all that animal rearing and slaughter, all those days at markets prodding hapless sheep and unhappy cows with their sticks which rubs away at their regard for any humanity beyond their rustic club.

It happened one Friday morning. I was off school for some reason, and playing out in the front garden, making a new batch of arrows with garden canes. Our family dog, Major, who had been with us through all our adventures since Wymersley Road, was 'helping' by chasing around with sticks in his jaws. He was a typical family Labrador; affectionate, faithful, gentle, but above all, protective. The main farmhouse where our landlord lived was about half a mile along a lane which ran at the side of our home. The farmer was, like his predecessor at the other side of the valley, a surly, humourless man, the same ruddy face, flat cap and green clothing. Is there a place where all farming types shop? What is it with oiled Berber jackets, beige shirts, olive hats and scarves and agricultural overalls – are they all some kind of camouflage to blend their wearers into the landscape?
So frequently our landlord would cut across the un-fenced, open end of our garden on his tractor, caring not a jot for the way his huge rear wheels churned up the grass. Having completed a few new arrows, I was about to let one fly to see how good my pigeon-feather flights were, when the tractor suddenly rumbled into view, coughing large clouds of diesel smoke. It was travelling faster than I anticipated as I pulled back my bowstring. The arrow flew straight and hit the farmer on his leg. Naturally, they were simply blunt toys, sharpened at one end with my pencil sharpener, so they would stand no chance of puncturing regular clothing. The arrow bounced off his leg, and he slammed the brakes on.
He sat on the growling tractor, casting such a malevolent stare in my direction that I froze.

"Sorry mister. Didn't mean to – "
But he dropped down from his mechanical steed and walked towards me, shouting.

"You bloody Gyppo! You could've had me eye out wi'that! Where's 'yer mother?"
So loud and threatening was his voice that Major, who was crouched in front of me, suddenly leaped in his direction and sank his teeth into the top of his wellington. It looked very funny; the dog hadn't drawn blood, simply rubber, yet he was shaking the farmer's leg like a fox would shake a cockerel.

"Git this mad mutt off me! Gerroff, y'bloody mongrel!"
Mam appeared, wiping her hands on her apron. She shouted at Major and he let go of his victim and went to her side, yet still regarding him with snarls and bared teeth. The farmer was suitably shaken, but I was glad.

"Not only are your bloody *picaninnies* dangerous," he barked, pointed at me, "firing bloody arrows at passers by, but y've a mad dog here and I'll not have it on my land!"
As I pondered over being referred to as a 'picaninny', Mam busied herself apologising profusely, but he was having none of it.

"I've a bloody mind to get rid of the lot of you and let this house to some decent people. You and your kids are –"
Mam, on the verge of tears, cut him short.

"My kids are what? They're *kids* for Christ's sake! They play, they don't mean any harm. Why are you threatening us with eviction? Don't your own dogs protect you?"
He coughed and then spat on the grass.

"My dogs are under control. So, if you want a roof over your head, you'll have this dangerous animal put down. If it isn't, then you'll be out of here in a month."
Mam was now in tears.

"So, because a dog nips your welly, he has to die. Will that make you happy, then? He's a family pet! Or would you like me to put the kids down as well?"
He began to walk back to the tractor, then paused and turned,

pointing at the still snarling Major.

"If you don't get rid of it, I'll come round here and shoot the bugger. And then y'can all pack up and clear off. This is *my* house, *my* land, and I have my rights!"

And so it came to pass that I was appointed Major's executioner. Major was my friend, often my companion when there was no-one to play with. But so fraught and insecure was our situation, and so raw and strained Mam's nervous disposition since arriving in this difficult valley, that her reason had begun to leave her. Dad was out at work, and I only wished that he'd been there. The farmer wouldn't have stood a chance.

After a while, as I sat there on a log with Major at my side, I had hoped that she wouldn't over-react to the event. But no. A few minutes later she came out with Major's lead in one hand and her purse in the other. She clipped his lead onto his collar and handed it to me. She then opened her purse and took out a ten shilling note. She was sobbing, in tears.

"Go down into town. In the road around the corner from the tobacconist's shop there's a big shed where the dustmen park their lorries. That's where they deal with unwanted cats and dogs."

A shiver ran through me. "What? But we *want* Major!"

"I know, I know," she sobbed, tears rolling down her face.

"But I'm frightened, son. It's hard enough living in this dump as it is, but winter's come and if we get chucked out, what will we do? Oh, God, I'm sorry, I'm so sorry, but take Major to the Corporation shed, I think this money will be enough, and they'll put Major to sleep."

Put him to *sleep*? The words bounced around in my mind.

"How long for?" I asked.

"Oh, son – it means forever. He'll go to dog heaven and it'll be a better place than this. I wish I could go as well."

The more I remonstrated, the more adamant she became. I had no choice. I had to obey my parents and that was that. I too was now in tears as I set off down through the gorse and heather with poor Major tethered to my side. We would pause every few yards, his tail wagging, and I would stoop down and hug him. And I knew that there was something in his eyes; something knowing, a doleful look of fear and puzzlement. It took over thirty minutes to reach town and eventually we arrived at the tall, asbestos-roofed corporation depot. Suddenly, Major halted in his tracks, sat back on his haunches and howled. He *knows*! I thought, oh, God! He knows!

I had to virtually drag him into the cavernous building and a tall, pipe-smoking man wearing a leather jerkin appeared from behind the parked refuse trucks. He looked at me and then at the dog. I was still crying. He placed a gentle hand on my shoulder, then stooped down to our level and stroked Major.

"Now, now, sonny. You look upset. What're y'doing in here, then?" I could hardly get the words out between staccato bouts of sobbing.

"This is Major. He's our dog. He's been naughty and bitten a farmer, and my Mam's sent him here because he has to be put to sleep." I held up the ten shilling note.

"Is this enough money?"

I could see how sympathetic the man was. He sighed and shook his head.

"Oh, aye, it's only half a crown. Are you sure about this?" I nodded, still sobbing.

"If we don't do it then the farmer's going to chuck us out," I said. He took Major's lead and we walked over to the side of the building to a steel rectangular tank, about the size of a large coffin, with a heavy sealed lid. It had pipes going into it. Major whimpered.

"Now, son, this is where the cats and dogs, and sometimes other animals, go to heaven. It doesn't hurt them. They go to sleep and soon they're all happy. And don't worry, because in many years time, when we all go to heaven, we'll meet up with our pets again. So, he's really going on a nice holiday."

I appreciated his efforts at consolation, but I was in such a state of grief by this time, I could have easily asked him to send me to heaven as well. Major suddenly became calm, wagged his tail, and I gave him one last hug as he licked my face. The man then unfastened his lead, picked him up bodily and lowered him into the steel coffin, and closed the lid. He then turned some valves on the pipes and I stood there for a moment, staring at this destructive apparatus, wondering what evil genius had committed it to the drawing board.

We walked away, the man taking me by my hand, Major's lead hanging limply in my other. At a kind of rostrum-cum-desk by the wall, the man took out a brass cash box and a receipt book. He gave me seven shillings and sixpence change and a receipt, which read *'disposing of one dog, 2/6d.'*

The death of Major was a turning point. On my sorry way back home that tragic day I sought some strength in my visions of Crazy Horse. What would the death of a mere dog have been to him? He had seen whole villages of men, women and little children ripped apart by the U.S. Infantry. He had fought and killed time and time again. He had courage. Yet here was I, sobbing my way through the rough grass over a dog sent to the happy hunting ground. I realised that Uncle Charlie had been correct – 'You'll never be an Indian as long as you've got a hole in your arse." Dad wasn't a pioneer after all, and I wasn't a Sioux.

Mam never forgave herself for letting her emotions get the better of her. And in a small way, I never forgave her for making me do it. It did not affect our mutual love; yet no eleven year old should have ever had to perform such a traumatic task. With Dad finding regular work hard to come by, things at home were not improving. Fierce arguments raged between Mam and Dad every night and Alexander and I lay listening to them in bed in the cold darkness wondering what the outcome of all this might be. Yet we thoroughly understood the thrust behind it all. Mam had become so unhappy, nervous and depressed. She blamed everything on Dad's somewhat rash decision to head west in his dreams to become a smallholder. He was a good joiner and carpenter, but he had as much chance of being a farmer as I had of being Crazy Horse. It was a dream. Perhaps he was, after all, Auntie Flo's 'gunner', but he tried, oh, how he tried. Sadly the truth was we had been given a fine new house back in our home town, with the new life that went with it, but we had squandered that chance and Dad's compensation money in exchange for almost two years of medieval misery.

During November there was much activity, with letters being written and received, and Dad making frequent trips to Mrs. McCready's to use her telephone. As December approached, when I came home from school one night, bearing a dish of shepherd's pie I had made in the cookery class, Mam sat us all down and told us what was going on.

"Your dad has an Auntie Sally in Hull. She has an old building at the back of her house where they used to keep horses. We're going to ask her to store all our furniture there, and Dad says his aunt will put us up until he finds a job and we find somewhere to live."

"What does this mean?" I asked.

"It means," she replied, "that we're leaving this awful place and going back where we belong - to Hull."

❖ ❖ ❖ ❖

Crazy Horse and The Coalman

PART FOUR:

THE HOOP IS BROKEN

Crazy Horse and The Coalman

10:
TO THE END
OF THE EARTH

'And I, to whom so great a vision was given in my youth, you see me now a pitiful old man who has done nothing, for the nation's hoop is broken and scattered.'

Black Elk, Sioux Holy Man.

In 1888, eleven years after the murder of Crazy Horse, the Sioux, penned in on their reservations and bombarded with yet more land-grabbing treaties, had become little more than a sideshow, a brave memory on the Plains. Yet they were still far from 'tame', and their wildness was much in demand in another area – the new phenomenon of the Wild West Show.

Colonel William Cody, known as Buffalo Bill, was the king of Wild West showmen. I learned that his huge entourage of cowboys, sharp-shooters, horses, cattle and buffalo – and, thrilling to me – plains Indians, had at least twice set up camp on Hull's traditional fairground on Walton Street.

Later in life, I researched more into Cody's Hull visits, and unearthed two remarkable stories. At the end of one visit, towards the end of the 19th century, when loading the Wilson Line steamers in Hull's docks, ready to travel back across the Atlantic to their native land, a number of buffaloes panicked on the dockside and escaped along Hull's Hedon Road. Cody despatched wranglers and Indians on horseback to round the poor beasts up. The thought of the Sioux and various whooping cowboys racing through the streets of my home town on a buffalo hunt filled me with amazement. It still does. Yet there were other stories which put my hero people onto my native soil.

Chief Long Wolf, a veteran of the Sioux wars was buried in Brompton Cemetery on June 13, 1892. He was 59, and died of bronchial pneumonia when touring with Buffalo Bill's Wild West Show. Also in his grave rested an Indian girl named Star Ghost Dog, who had died just 17 months old after she had fallen from her mother's arms as they rode together on horseback. In 1997 a British woman, Elizabeth Knight, tracked down Long Wolf's family in the Black Hills in South Dakota. Long Wolf's remains were taken home, and he now lies in the ancestral burial ground of the Oglala Sioux tribe, the Wolf Creek Community Cemetery at Pine Ridge. He had a great grandson, John Black Feather, who commented;

"Back then, they had burials at sea, they did ask his wife if she wanted to take him home and she figured that as soon as they hit the water they would throw him overboard, so that's why they left him in England."

Yet in 1888, there were others lost in a strange land. After their final well-attended performance in Manchester, the Buffalo Bill show decamped to Hull where they would board the Wilson steamers and head home. The Sioux, more than any cowboys, were extremely prone to homesickness. Yet Cody paid well and had a genuine rapport and an affection for the Indians, and many great braves and chiefs travelled with him around Europe, including Sitting Bull. He would drink and eat with them after a show, and often slept in their tipis.

On that day in question in 1888, three Lakota Sioux, led by the legendary holy man, Black Elk, became lost on the streets of Hull. By the time they found the docks, the tide had gone and their compatriots with it. Only one of the three spoke any English. They knew they were stranded, with only their wages for the last performance. Somehow, with the help of a number of slightly amazed Hull people, somewhat fazed to come across full-blooded American Indians in their native costume wandering around the city, they managed to find Paragon Station and bought tickets to London. There they joined another Wild West show, Mexican Pete's, yet had to serve another full year throughout Europe on a dollar a day before they would finally run into their old boss again in Paris in 1889.

In France, Cody threw a party for Black Elk and his companions, gave him $90 and a steamer ticket back to New York. After two winters away from his people, Black Elk, whose father was a contemporary of Crazy Horse who knew him well, arrived home, to find that the plight of his corralled, starving people was even worse than when he had left. Yet Black Elk has left us a great legacy. In 1932 the writer John G. Neidhardt met the great man, then well over 100 years old, at Pine Ridge, and after many long conversations wrote his story in the classic book, *Black Elk Speaks*. And to think – he walked the streets, albeit briefly, of my home town.

My Dad knew that leaving Mytholmroyd was some kind of surrender. As a military man it was something he'd never had to do before. Yet his enemy now had been his own inability to grasp his dream firmly enough and make it work. Contrary to what Margaret Thatcher would later preach, we were not all budding entrepreneurs and potential wealth-makers. The only 'trickle down' effect we enjoyed came from leaking roofs. We were naïve, simple people weaned on fantasies.

It was now late November and the logistics of moving our furniture and then ourselves, separately, were not simple. We had planned to travel back to Hull by train via Leeds on the Friday. On the previous Wednesday, the furniture van arrived from Hull and found its way to our remote hovel with some difficulty. Yet it was nice once again to hear those Hull accents. The driver, a burly man in bib and brace overalls, stood in our dark, miserable hallway and looked around. He knew where we were from and that we were going back there.

"Bloody hell ... it's like summat out of Charles Dickens. How the 'ell have you lived here?"

"With a lot of struggle," replied Mam, cradling Patrick in her arms. Later in the afternoon, we were standing in an empty house with nothing but some blankets, a few cardboard boxes, some cracked teacups and a pan of water boiling on the fire. The removal men, armed with our Auntie Sally's address off Woodcock Street in Hull, wished us luck and set off. For the next two severely miserable nights, we slept on sheets of cardboard, wrapping ourselves in blankets. On the Friday, with Dad carrying a suitcase and Mam some clothes in carrier bags with Patrick in his tansad, we set off in a bitter winter wind for Halifax.

I had a soft spot for Halifax, because it was there I began to realise that I had another interest beyond the Sioux; the sea. It had begun, as many of my inspirations had, in the cinema, with the release of Walt Disney's *20,000 Leagues Under The Sea*. During its Halifax run I had seen the film three times. I was fascinated by James Mason as the brooding Captain Nemo, and the silent, mysterious obedience of his crew on board the *Nautilus*. And, of course, the movie starred two of our favourite stars – Peter Lorre and Kirk Douglas. I had the comic, the picture book, and the Jules Verne novel. There would be nothing as riveting as this until I ran into John Huston's *Moby Dick* a couple of years later.

As the bus passed the Halifax cinema on our way to the station I was overcome by a sudden wave of doom and nausea. Yes, we were going to Hull, but to what? Who was this mysterious Auntie Sally and what would it be like living with her? Then the thought of yet another school loomed. Still, there was a train journey to look forward to.

We had to wait for a connection to Hull in Leeds so Dad took us all to the station buffet where we had ham sandwiches and a cup of tea. As ever, his indefatigable optimism had resurfaced, and for a while, even Mam, who had been feeding Patrick on her knee, seemed to cheer up.

There was always something special about arriving in Hull by train. This sense of homecoming was certified when we passed a familiar advertisement pained on the wall at the end of a block of houses. It was for a furniture store, Turners, and read *'Everything But The Girl'*. We staggered tired and dazed into Hull's Paragon Station just before 8.30 pm, and went to catch the 70 trolley bus to Hessle Road, the heart of Hull's fishing community. I was tired, we all were, and poor little Patrick was in desperate need of a nappy change. There was quite a whiff emanating from the Tansad. Yet it felt good to be back home; the familiar smell of fish from the docks, familiar streets, drunken trawlermen, and the Hull voices all around us. Yet all I wanted was to sleep.

It was dark and bitterly cold as we made our way down the Boulevard and onto Woodcock Street. Eventually, we reached our destination. Woodcock Street's houses formed a continuous terrace, punctuated here and there by the odd set of double doors signifying a one-time tradesman's residence. Such a place was Auntie Sally's. We stood shivering on the pavement as Dad knocked on her door. We were about to discover that Dad's reading of character and excessive optimism had been at play yet again.

Sally was a small, mousy-haired woman wearing a gingham pinny and smoking a cigarette. She looked Dad up and down then glanced disdainfully at us.

"So. You made it, then."

"Aye, did the furniture come OK?" asked Dad.

"Aye – it's stored in the old stable, like I said. When do you want it?"

"Well – I need to find a job first, and, well, I was hoping you could put us up for a couple of nights until we get sorted?"

Exasperated, Mam prodded Dad in the back.

"I thought this was all sorted out?"

Sally looked at Mam.

"Don't trust this bugger to sort anything out. He never

mentioned anything. The furniture's as far as I'm going."
Mam lowered her head and put her hand to her eyes. My heart had already sunk.

"But..." said Dad, in his best pleading tone, "look at us – we've a little bairn here been travelling all day. It's gone nine o'clock and we've nowhere to go."

Sally shrugged. "And whose fault's *that*? Not mine. You ought to take more care of your family, Stanley. Now, I'm getting cold standing here, so I'll say good night."

At that the door slammed shut.

We stood beneath the gas streetlamp, a forlorn, tatty tableau reminiscent of sad characters in a silent Charlie Chaplin film. Mam was crying, then Patrick started up, and Alexander gripped my freezing hand with his and said

"I'm tired. Can we go to bed now?"

"So," said Mam, temporarily composing herself, "any big ideas? Which street are we sleeping on? Maybe there's a graveyard somewhere – let's face it, we might as well all be bloody *dead*!"

Dad fished in his coat pocket and produced some coins. Ahead was the junction of Woodcock Street and St. George's Road. He started walking and, with no other choice, we all followed. At the junction stood one of Hull's white telephone boxes.

"Now," he said, still trying to sound positive, "it's not as bad as it looks. I know an old army mate who's on the phone, and he's got a holiday caravan. I'll see if he can put us up."

He spent some minutes going through the phone book, then made his call. We couldn't quite hear what he was saying, but we could hear that pleading tone again. Eventually, he put the phone down and emerged, smiling.

"Right. It's all fixed. He only lives three streets from here, so we'll all go up to Hessle Road, you all wait by the trolley bus stop while I go and get the keys."

"Aye, well," said Mam, wide-eyed, "so where's this caravan then?"

"Hornsea." said Dad, as he ambled along three paces ahead of us.

"*Hornsea?*" wailed Mam, "but it's gone nine o'clock and that's over an hour's bus ride!"

We reached the Hessle Road trolley stop and Dad actually went off running at great speed. We stood freezing outside a well-lit furniture shop as the trolley buses came and went. After what seemed like an hour, but was only perhaps twenty minutes, Dad came running along the pavement, gasping for breath, just as a trolley bus pulled up. In his hand he held a bunch of keys.

The last East Yorkshire Motor Services bus to the distant seaside resort of Hornsea was just about to depart from the Paragon bus station as we all clambered on board. I began to wonder how more bizarre this epic could get before the chimes of midnight. We had travelled across Yorkshire by bus, two trains, two trolley buses and now this journey into the unknown depths of Holderness. Yes, Hornsea was a very nice little day-trip watering hole for a family at the height of summer. With its beautiful inland lake, the Mere, it was the social superior to its nearby sister resort, the more down-market Withernsea, but I did not relish being at either place in the dark at the tail end of an icy November.

As the bus trundled on through villages, dropping off passengers, Mam simply sat in silence, red-eyed, staring through the window at the black, heartless night outside. Eventually it drew to a halt at around 11.15 pm on the Hornsea promenade, and we all piled out. By this time poor little Patrick's bum cheeks must have been welded together with the vulcanised issue of about ten hours of infant poo.

The first thing which hit us on alighting from the bus was the razor-edged, bitter icy wind raging off the nearby North Sea. As the bus vanished en route to some warm night garage, we were left standing outside the shut-down Corrigan's Amusement arcade, with nothing between us but a few yards of grass and an angry ocean, the only people in this

desolate town crazy enough to be at large on such a foul night.
Dad stood in the doorway of the arcade and lit a match, looking at an address on a slip of paper. Even then he was smiling his positive smile.

"Right. It's on the south cliff camp, Avenue eight, plot five. Follow me."

We had to pass along the promenade's sea front to make our way to the south cliffs, and the waves were so violent, powering up the deserted beach like an angry herd of horses in the frosty darkness, that they flung sharp darts of icy spray into our tired faces. Yet onward we shuffled. Patrick was now wailing. I looked around the low horizon at the sleeping town, and to my amazement, noticed in the odd window here and there something which made me want to weep. Christmas tree lights. It was then I reminded myself – yes, Yuletide was less than four weeks away. I began to wish I was Jewish.

It seemed a steep climb along a muddy path onto the cliff tops but eventually we reached the 'camp'.
In the 21st century, urban civilisation, with its laws and regulations, health and safety, has built up a body of legal supervision around holiday sites and caravans. As far as I recall, none of this existed in 1954. In those post-war years everything and anything could become a 'holiday home'. This included de-commissioned single and double decker buses, clapped out furniture vans, abandoned World War 2 gliders, crashed bombers, and especially defunct Pullman railway carriages. However, as we struggled through the wind-lashed blackness, we eventually found that our berth of punishment was not in any of these luxury brackets. Yes, it had a name; *Mon Repose*. It was, however, two British
Railways goods wagons joined together with some windows cut out and filled with Perspex. As Dad unlocked the huge, rusty Bulldog lock and slid the door open, I heard Mam gasp.

"Bloody hell...so it's come to *this*..."

I suppose that first night in the wagons would have been familiar to anyone hired as an extra for *Schindler's List*.

Once we'd managed to get inside and shut out the howling wind, which now bore flakes of snow, we examined our new abode with the illuminating aid of a box of matches. Dad spotted the oil lamps first and soon we could see more clearly. Everything felt cold and damp. Dad's mystery army friend had done the best he could with what were, essentially, covered cattle trucks. It was probably heaven in the height of July and August, but now, in November, it seemed like a dungeon. There was a cast iron stove, and partitions at either end with sliding doors so that the central area was the kitchen/dining/living room with a bedroom at each end. There were pictures on the walls of sunny scenes from the Yorkshire Dales and sailing ships. I began to think that life as a galley boy on the *Cutty Sark* would be a doddle compared to this. As for the rural Yorkshire life, I'd had quite enough of that, thank you very much. Alexander and I claimed the room with two beds in it and Mam and Dad would share the double bedded room with Patrick. There was a paraffin stove, which was fortunately full, which he lit and placed in the double bed area with the feeble hope of drying it out. We were relieved to discover pile of logs by the rusty stove and a bucket of coal, so we soon got a fire going. Bleak and basic though it all seemed, I was highly relieved to at least be *somewhere*.

Holding aloft a flickering lamp, Dad searched around outside, where there was a kind of lean-to made up of old pine doors. He tried the keys and managed to open this, and discovered a five gallon drum of paraffin, plus more coal and wood. Water came from a standpipe outside by the sliding doors. On the draining board next to the old stone sink was a primus stove, and we soon had a kettle of water on the boil. Mam was then, at long last, able to perform the grim task of prising Patrick out of his ordure-encrusted nappy. We found a bucket and had to stand the offending brown article outside.

Sadly, we had nothing to eat, other than a packet of Rich Tea biscuits. We had two each and Mam said she had to keep the rest to feed little Patrick. We did have a cup of tea, but having eaten nothing for nine hours since a British Railways ham sandwich at Leeds, we were ravenous. Eventually, still in our clothes and shivering beneath the inadequate summer bedding, which felt wet and smelled like compost, we all fell into a deep sleep which even the roaring North Sea gale would not disturb. That night I dreamed I was back at Wymersley Road, on the golf course with Gilbert, playing Crazy Horse games. I dreamed of Crazy Horse sleeping in his tipi in his winter camp, and of sitting next to Barbara at school, of golf balls, plates of ham and potato patties, Dan Dare and PC 49.

When I awoke much of the cold dampness had gone. It's amazing what body heat will do. Sunlight was streaming in through the Perspex window, and I could hear the waves crashing on the nearby beach. Alexander was still asleep and I looked around the tiny compartment with its hardboard-lined damp-stained walls and little framed pictures. Was this, then, to be our life? Had we surrendered to primitive stone cottages, nasty farmers, horrible schools, condemned dogs, unfriendly aunts, and now – this? A hard cold bed in a goods wagon? Where next – a cave in the hills?

Dad had been up early and had lit the stove, and when I wandered into the living area it felt dry and warm. The kettle had boiled and he was making tea, although we had no milk and sugar. He looked at me and smiled.

"Big adventure, eh, son?"

Well, I thought, if this is your idea of an adventure, count me out. Adventures had plots and excitement. They weren't supposed to involve maximum misery. I remained silent. He handed me a cup of steaming black tea.

"You take this into your Mam and tell her I'm going to find a shop and get us some groceries. If the fire goes down, put some coal on – but not too much – we'll have to be careful. I'll be back as soon as I can."

We really needed a wash and a change of clothes, but whilst Mam tried to tidy herself up and feed Patrick some mushed-up biscuits in warm tea, Alexander and I decided to go out and explore our new seaside environment.

What struck me first was the sheer desolation. In July and August this place would have been buzzing with family life, kids running to the beach, people sitting outside in deck chairs. Now, with its thin dusting of early snow, the black hulks of the locked converted buses, gliders and railway carriages, interspersed here and there by 'proper' caravans, reminded me of an elephant's graveyard. The only sound was the wind and the sea. I realised that on this site, probably around 20 acres, and well away from the prim and proper housing of the town, we were the only human beings.

Alexander and I stood shivering on the cliff top, staring out at the churning grey ocean. We found a series of steps cut into the muddy cliff face with a timber handrail and ventured down onto the beach. We threw stones into the waves, and ran from the white, advancing foam.

"I like the seaside," said Alexander.

"I do," I said, "but not like this. Nobody comes here when it's winter."

"We've come here, though," he said, "is this a holiday?"

I threw a large stone and sighed.

"No. It's like being in prison."

Over the next few days we managed some kind of 'settling in' and began eating again, although preparing meals with no oven and a single primus stove proved quite a challenge for Mam. I missed the radio badly. It had been stored in Hull with our furniture, and the rest of our clothing. Dad tried to find a coal man who would deliver to the site, but the local merchant refused, so Dad had to make two trips into town with the Tansad returning with two bags of coal.

I watched him one afternoon struggling up the muddy road along the cliff top and I almost cried at his image. He looked, from a distance, pushing this tiny pram top-heavy with its unwieldy load, like some World War 2 European refugee. Later that day I would have to help him with the unpleasant task of emptying the outside Elsan toilet. The contents had to be carried to a nearby cesspit, which was, thankfully, frozen.

Despite the occasional snow flurry, the winter weather stayed bright and sunny, and Alexander and I, wearing every item of clothing Mam had managed to stuff into our suitcase and carrier bags, went for long walks along the deserted beach. But the next week the horror of school arrived.

If I had thought that school in Hebden Bridge seemed slightly middle class, I was in for a shock in Hornsea. The town is a very pleasant place, one which, in my present life, I would be quite happy to live in. I might generalise, yet it always seemed the domain of teachers and solicitors, professional people. Perhaps it was the additional beauty and sophistication of its marvellous inland lake, Hornsea Mere, the largest natural inland water area in Yorkshire. That alone would make it a desirable place to live and push up property prices. Yet in my poverty-stricken *untermensch* childhood incarnation, it was the last place on earth I wished to be.

Alexander was lucky – he was packed off to an infant school. I arrived with Mam at the school of my 11 year old peers. I can't remember its name – it was mentally erased. We first met the headmaster who seemed somewhat bemused by our situation. He insisted that I wore the school blazer and cap. I've no idea where Dad got the money from for this, as we had been off Uncle Ken's money-lending radar for almost
two years, although he would soon be cleaning up from us again. Yet the first Monday I turned up at the new school wearing the blazer, with badge, and cap. Pity about the 8th Army khaki shorts and the baggy socks, though, hardly enhanced by the wellingtons. I was regarded in class by the

snooty, well-dressed kids as something of an oddity, and at playtime was asked the familiar question 'are you a gypsy?'
So I kept to myself, worked hard in English lessons, failed stupendously in maths, avoided PE with fake notes purporting to be from my Mam. Then one Friday afternoon, our teacher, a middle-aged ex-forces type with a handlebar moustache, asked me to stay behind at 4 pm.

"Now then, Bainton. When did you last get your hair cut?" I could not help but think what a peculiar and outrageous question this was.

"Can't remember, sir." He looked me up and down with a blend of pity and distaste.

"Well, I can quite believe that. You see, we have certain standards at this school and we don't like our boys to be scruffy, so you'd better tell your parents that your hair needs cutting."

"Yes, sir. Can I go now?" He waved me out of the room.
My hair was longer than I'd ever had it before, but I welcomed it being almost over my ears and on my shirt collar, because it was cold on that beach and its extra padding complemented the cosiness of my balaclava.

"He said *what*?" said Mam, outraged when I told her about the hair cut.

"He said he didn't like boys being scruffy."

"I'll give him *scruffy*," she barked, "the cheeky sod!" and for one horrible moment I imagined that she might storm the school dining hall as she had done in Hebden Bridge with Mr. Lister and his 'piggie' outburst. Although I greatly appreciated her courageous protection, a similar event at this new school was something I could do without.

"Right. Well if your teacher thinks we can go forking money out for barbers, with your Dad still out of work, then he's got another think coming. We can sort your hair out here, on our own. We've got some scissors and a comb."
That night, after a tea of sausages and beans, I was sat on a box by the stove and in the light from a smoking oil lamp.

Mam proceeded to cut my hair. It was a painful process, with my ears being nipped at least twice by the chattering scissors. I began to wish for a mirror to see how this was coming along, because just when I thought Mam had finished, she stood back and sighed and said

"Mmm – still patchy round the back and sides. I know what we'll do ..." At that, she went to the cupboard beneath the sink and produced a large pudding basin. This was duly plonked onto my head. I've always had a big head and the rim of the basin rested a good two inches above my ears. Mam kept on clipping, clipping, then said to Dad

"Have you got a new blade in your razor?" He reached over to the sink and produced his sturdy Gillette safety razor. Mam then proceeded to strip away what stubble was left by raking the blade along the now bare, cold exposed areas of my cranium. Where the blade nicked, (in several places) Dad was on hand to apply cigarette papers. She removed the basin and held the oil lamp aloft.

"That should keep them happy."

When I looked in the small mirror on the wall in our bedroom area, the word 'happy' became far from suitable. Looking back at me was a junior vision of a 13th century monk.

The ancient history of the severe tonsure is vague. However, shaving your hair off in a religious order probably resulted from the odd notion that long hair is the mark of a freeman, so the monastic 'slave' needed an over-the-top haircut to denote he was a servant of God. A wilder idea is that tonsure mimics male pattern baldness and thus lends artificial respectability to younger, hairier males. Yes, a nasty haircut seems sensible and fine for a soldier or a Buddhist or Trappist, but what I was about to have to live with would have had the Carthusians in fits of laughter. I had to admit, as I illuminated my cig-paper festooned bonce with a candle, that the demarcation line produced by the basin was dead neat. Where my hair ended, there began a desert of pink, scraped skin, and if my hair was going to look like this on the Monday morning at school, then I was in big trouble.

That Monday morning was a trauma too far. I had managed to keep my cap on in the assembly hall, even though two teachers had gestured to me to remove it. But when we were finally seated in the classroom for a geography lesson, I was aware that everyone was looking at me. Then the teacher pointed with his ruler.
"You're the new lad, Bainton, is it?"
"Yes sir."
"Well, I don't know how you were brought up, but here we do not wear our hats indoors, it is bad manners, so remove your cap at once."
"I'd rather not sir."
The space between my response and his steady approach between the desks had an ambience reminiscent of that horrible pause between Oliver Twist asking for more and the Beadle's explosion. He arrived at my desk and whipped away my hat. The look on his face was classic. It was a combined expression of surprised horror and shock. Then the class erupted into laughter, with two wags nearby chanting 'Friar Tuck! Friar Tuck!" I grabbed my cap, got up from my desk, pushed past the teacher and ran all the way 'home'.

With Christmas holidays almost upon us, Mam agreed that I need not go back to school until January, when it was hoped that some of my hair might grow back. She did take me to a barber eventually, but he simply threw his head back and chortled "Blimey! Never seen anything like that! It's too far gone for me to sort out!"

I think the Christmas of 1954 was one of the poorest I can remember. Mam had become ill, bed-ridden with pneumonia. The doctor blamed our accommodation, but Mam refused to go into hospital. She seemed to improve a little on Christmas day.

But what a sad day that was. In my Christmas pillow case was a Mars bar, an ex-army jack knife, some comics, and, because I'd left mine in Mytholmroyd, a new bow and three arrows. Alexander got some clockwork cars and jelly babies. Patrick got his nappy changed – again. Our Christmas dinner did include a small Christmas pudding, but the main course was a plate of Irish stew and a slice of bread. During the afternoon Alexander and I went onto the beach. I tried out my bow and arrows, pulled the bow back too far and snapped it in two. To overcome this disappointment, I began throwing the jack knife, blade open, into the sand. After three satisfying throws, the fourth hit a stone and the blade snapped off. So we sat in silence on a clump of fallen cliff, me eating my Mars bar, Alexander chewing his jelly babies.

After heavy snow in January Mam said she could take no more. Some days she'd be in bed, others, she'd be pale, pottering around, sad and worried. Dad had found building work in Hull but it was taking its toll. To get to the city by 8 am he had to rise at 5.30, and then make his way to the promenade for the early bus, and he never arrived home at night until after seven. But then, one night, he brought good news. He had another aunt who lived close by the fish docks in Scarborough Street on Hessle Road. He'd been to see her and asked if she could put us up until we could find a rented house. Mam was curious as to why he'd never thought of this other relative on that awful night when Auntie Sally turned us away. His response was curious.

"Well ... Auntie Gladys is a difficult woman."
"And Sally wasn't?" queried Mam.
"No – look; she's a lot older than Sally, and her husband, my Uncle Bill, well – I've had to work on him to bring him round. We can't stay here until the spring – this place is going to be for holidaymakers then, but if we go to Auntie Gladys's, it'll only be for a few weeks at the most. And she could do with the money. We'll soon find somewhere to rent, and this travelling every day's wearing me out."

I always wondered why we never approached any of Mam's family to help us out, but I think it was a matter of her pride and Dad's responsibility. With no furniture and again, just our suitcase and carrier bags, moving from Hornsea was simply a couple of bus rides. Yet we were all getting tired of the misery, the uncertainty. Mam had no idea who Gladys and Bill were, and neither had I. Sadly, we were about to find out.

❖ ❖ ❖ ❖

11: FISH AND FLEAS

*'There we found a Cheyenne cannot live.
So we came home. Better it was, we thought,
To die fighting than to perish of sickness...
It is only when the hearts of the Women are in the mud,
that the People are destroyed.'*

**Dull Knife, (a.k.a. Morning Star) Cheyenne
1810-1883**

On December 16th 1876 Crazy Horse, realising that the euphoria of annihilating Custer the previous year had evaporated, decided to see if a different approach might benefit his hungry people. He took his camp to the Tongue River, hoping that they might find food and mercy. He organised for eight of his warriors to go as peace envoys, all carrying white flags of surrender, to Colonel Nelson 'Bearcoat' Miles's powerful infantry encampment on the Tongue River, later known as Fort Keogh. As Crazy Horse watched from the hilltop, five of his envoys were gunned down to die in the snow in minutes. There was no chance to parley. This only confirmed to the chief that the white man offered nothing but treachery. His band broke camp and headed back to a bitter, starving winter on the Plains. Yet retribution and revenge for Little Big Horn ruled the ranks of blue. When Bearcoat Miles (so called by the Indians because of the bearskin coat he wore) had pursued and destroyed the fleeing Crazy Horse camp and all their food supplies in January 1877, the children starved and many froze to death. Crazy Horse knew He could no longer prevent his people from approaching the new reservations and Indian agencies. It was that or death.

As Luther Standing Bear commented: "Crazy Horse saw nothing, knew nothing but treachery from the white man. He felt himself above dealing with men who knew no honour. As by all such men Crazy Horse was sincerely hated and feared."

As we arrived in Hull that March day my thoughts went back to Crazy Horse. In his last few years, moving on, breaking camp, and setting up camp, hunting for game, which was diminishing, as were the buffalo, which the white hunters had destroyed in their thousands. The Lakota Sioux and their allies were facing nothing but abject misery. Of course, we too seemed always on the move but our experiences were luxury compared to what the Sioux went through, yet their story remained imprinted on my young mind.

After we'd alighted from the trolley bus and began making our way to our new domicile on Scarborough Street, Dad seemed somewhat serious and quiet. His optimism, for a change, was not making an appearance. We reached Auntie Gladys's terraced house, and the front door led straight into the living room. It was a tiny place, with a dark, cramped kitchen, an outside WC in a small yard, and only two small bedrooms. However, it did have electricity, water and gas – and they even had a radio!
None of us took to Aunt Gladys. There was something spiky and aggressive about her. She was probably in her early 60s, and very old fashioned in her dress, with her grey hair pulled back in a tight bun and wearing a grubby, lace-edged apron and smoking a cigarette. She immediately put me in mind of Arthur Lucan, known to music hall and film fans as Old Mother Riley. But at least Old Mother Riley made us laugh. No such luck with Gladys. She showed us up to our room. It contained a double bed and one single bed, and a chest of drawers.
"Y'll all have t'sleep in 'ere 'cos that's all there is. I'll put kettle on and you can put your stuff in the drawers."

She went downstairs and we stood between the beds, Mam holding Patrick in her arms.

"Good God," she whispered, "It can't get any worse…"

The beds had old army blankets and some sheets, but they looked grey and crumpled. We looked out of the bedroom window and all we could see was the back yard below and a lot of other back yards, and towering above it all a fish smokehouse, with its sinister row of chimney cowls, like the bent heads of some smoky beast. In fact the smell of fish was almost overpowering. It was a nasal melange of haddock, cod and kippers, tinged with something rotten. This was, of course, all part of our Hull heritage and on warm nights in the city fish got up everyone's nose, not just those who lived by St. Andrew's Dock. We put our few clothes in the newspaper-lined drawers and made our way downstairs, where a welcome cup of tea awaited us. Gladys was sat in a tall, spindle backed Windsor chair by the black-leaded fire range, smoking.

"Have a chair. How long d'ye think y'll be 'ere?"

It wasn't what we might have called a welcome.

"Oh," smiled Dad, his optimism returning slowly, "I've already got a job and we're on the look out for a place to rent, so it ought not to be long."

That first night was one of double horror. We sent out for fish and chips at 6 pm, and as we were eating this Uncle Bill arrived home from work. He was a short, wiry man with thick grey hair, probably not far off retirement. He took off his coat, and he was dressed in a stained brown boiler suit. After being introduced, he stood there for a while staring at us. Apparently they were a childless couple, and neither of them had any rapport with kids. But what threw us all was the way he stank. It was one hell of a foul pong. He noticed me wincing and holding my nose as he passed by.

"Aye, get used to it, lad. That's the smell of good, honest graft. I've been in fish manure for thirty odd years, so it doesn't bother us, does it, Glad?"

Gladys nodded. I watched Bill removing his boiler suit and to my horror, as he unrolled the turn-ups, several wriggling maggots fell onto the greasy carpet. He stooped and picked them up one by one, then disappeared with them into the kitchen. Gladys seemed slightly amused by our expressions.

"Aye, he brings 'is work 'ome every night, Saves them maggots in a jar and sells 'em for fishin' bait."

We continued trying to eat our rapidly cooling cod and chips as Gladys reached into the cupboard by the fireplace and produced first a pint bottle of Mackeson Stout then a pint beer glass. The glass was one of the dirtiest, foulest drinking vessels on the face of the earth. Its inner surface was caked with years of dried stout froth, and as she held the open bottle to fill it up, she looked at us and said

"This glass was my mother's before me. It's a real stout glass and never been washed. That's the way to drink stout properly." This insanitary bit of folk wisdom seems to be of dubious provenance, and if they served ale in pubs in such a fashion, we'd be one step away from the plague.

By nine o'clock there was no sign of the radio being switched on so we all said our goodnights and, with great embarrassment, bumping into one another, began to disrobe in the cramped bedroom. Mam, Dad and Patrick occupied the double bed, with me and Alexander sleeping head-to-toe in the single. Tired though we were, we were not going to enjoy much sleep. The fleas saw to that. First it was our legs and ankles, then our backs, arms and bellies. They weren't just fleas, but super-fleas on steroids. Mam got up at one time and switched on the light, and sat there, angrily picking the little brown devils off the sheets. I began to long for a cold, damp goods wagon on the cliff tops.

The next day meant yet another new school. Alexander went to Scarborough Street Juniors and I was packed off to Somerset Street. However, at last I had entered an educational establishment where most of the kids were as poor as, if not poorer, than us. I was no longer a gypsy. We were all gypsies. On Hessle Road, we had met our economic peers.

I quite liked the teachers, too. My form teacher was a wonderful man, an ex-RAF pilot called Mick Brown. He was tall, self-assured and did not suffer fools gladly, yet we knew he was one of the good guys. Some afternoons he would read to us from various collections of short stories, and in particular *The Little World of Don Camillo* by Giovanni Guareschi. These were stories about a priest who had been a resistance fighter in World War 2, when he had fought alongside his fellow partisan, the mayor of his village. The difference between the two men was that Don Camillo was a Catholic and the mayor was a communist. I never understood some parts of the stories, yet the way Mr. Brown read them was totally engaging and we all looked forward to this treat. With the number of trawler men's sons in our class we had a few real hard cases. Yet at last, here was a school where it didn't matter what we looked like or how we dressed. Our headmaster was a tough little man called Mr. Hannah, with a humorous penchant for sarcasm, and I think he had a false leg, or at least some wartime injury which made him walk with difficulty.

Yet what I noticed about these teachers is that they understood us. They were firm and fair. There was always trouble on swimming days. I particularly looked forward to these occasions. With our towels and trunks under our arms, supervised by the eagle-eyed Mick Brown, the whole class would be marched off along the vibrant, busy Hessle Road, with its brilliant collection of greengrocers and fruit shops, all setting their stalls out on the pavement. We would arrive at Madeley Street Baths at around 10 am, and have a brilliant time learning to swim. On the march back to school, the trouble sometimes started when at least two or three of the lads might steal an apple or orange when passing a stall. They were stupid to do it, because Mr. Brown always knew. Back in the classroom, just before the mid-day bell went, he would shout out the names of the miscreants, who would feign surprise or innocence. They would be called to the front of the class and receive six hefty whacks, three on each hand, from Mr. Brown's bamboo cane. To me, it seemed a steep price for a Granny Smith or a tangerine.

After a few flea-bitten, smelly weeks with Auntie Gladys and Uncle Bill, Mam had begun to put the pressure on Dad to find somewhere proper to live. I often wondered at his stoic resilience in living in the ways we had become used to. Perhaps, for man who'd fought and survived in the jungles of the Far East and bivouacked in the snowy corners of Europe, a bare stone cottage, a cold railway wagon or a flea-infested bed meant little. But Mam and her children had not been the recipients of good old British Army extreme survival training. We were domestic animals, and the 'domestic' part was beginning to slip away. Yes, we appreciated the old woman's compassion in taking us in, and Mam often told her so. It was indeed a welcome kindness. Yet we were so unhappy.

Then, at last, news came one night when he excitedly told us that he had come across a house to rent in Boynton Street, off the Boulevard. We kept the news from Gladys in case the deal might fail, yet it buoyed us all up immensely. I had also suffered a further disappointment living there. Gladys never seemed to have that radio on, which stood on the sideboard. One day, when she wasn't around, I tried to switch it on. It was dead. I asked her that night if it worked.

"Naw... last time that worked was for Churchill on VE Day. It needs valves. Anyway, there's nowt worth listenin' to." No, I thought – not for you, there isn't. The only culture in that house was in Bill's turn-ups.

Then one Saturday afternoon Mam did something which was bound to hasten our departure.

For some reason Gladys and Bill had gone out for the day, and we had the house to ourselves. The first thing Mam did was take all the bedding into the back yard, hang it on the washing line and beat seven bells out of it with a carpet beater.

Then she decided she would give the old house the thorough clean it so badly needed. She swept, dusted, scrubbed and polished until her hands were red, and with the front and back doors open and the breeze blowing though the house, it suddenly seemed so much better, even with the smell of fish. Once the bedding had been taken upstairs, she stood in the middle of the living room with her hands, business-like, on her hips. I noticed she was smiling.

"D'you *know* what I'm going to do?" she asked us.

"Nothing daft, I hope," said Dad.

She went over to Auntie Gladys's cupboard, and came away holding the encrusted, indecent stout glass.

"I'm going to *wash* this *filthy* thing!" she said.

Dad seemed to panic.

"Er – love – I don't think that's a good idea."

Mam thrust the rancid receptacle under his nose.

"Dirty old bitch! Smell it – go on, *smell it*! Oh *'that's the way to drink stout'* is it! Would you drink beer out of this in a pub? No. What kind of an example is that to these kids? It's a damned disgrace."

So she disappeared into the kitchen, boiled a kettle, and twenty minutes later emerged, polishing the old glass to crystal clarity with a tea towel. She placed it back in the cupboard and closed the door. Dad lowered his head. He looked pale. I had a feeling this was not going to play well. I was right.

On Saturday nights Gladys usually treated herself to not one but two bottles of Mackeson, and with the rent money Dad had been paying her, she could afford it. We had finished our tea of potted meat sandwiches and a Victoria sponge, when Gladys sat heavily down in her chair and reached for her cupboard. First she retrieved a bottle of stout, and then fumbled for the glass. She looked fazed and confused as she held it in her bony fingers. She looked at it in the way a Knight's Templar might have looked at his ultimate discovery – the Holy Grail.

Then she stood it on the hearth, got up, and began ferreting around in the cupboard. Dad looked away, shaking his head.

"Wha – where – where's me stout glass gone?"

She looked at Mam.

"Freda! What 'ave 'yer done wi' me *glass*?"

"It's there, Gladys – where you put it. On the hearth."

She sat back in her chair and picked up the sparkling glass.

"You ... you interfering *bitch!* This glass has never, ever been washed! And now you've ruined it! You've walked over my poor mother's grave!"

"Well," said Mam, quick as a flash, "if she'd been a bit cleaner she might have lasted a bit longer!"

Gladys put the glass back in the cupboard and glared at us all.

"I've had enough of the lot of you. I want you out of here – and if you're not gone in a fortnight, I'll have you chucked out!"

"Either that," said Mam, "or the bloody fleas'll *carry* us out!"

We had an early night that night, but there was quite an argument going on in the double bed.

Mam's faux pas with the stout glass was really the catalyst needed for Dad to do something positive. Our friendly loan shark, Uncle Ken, had tracked us down (or should I say Mam had tracked him down) and Mam took out a £40 loan. That was quite a big sum, and I know that the re-payment interest would have been huge. But it was needed. It went towards a deposit of rent on the house at 22 Boynton Street and it paid for the removal men to finally extricate our by now moth-eaten, cob-webbed furniture from Auntie Sally's dank stables. Another good thing for me was that we were moving less than half a mile, which meant I could stay at the same school, although Alexander would have to change yet again.

Leaving Aunt Gladys's house on a bright Spring Saturday morning was one of the happiest experiences we'd had for a long time. Mam did thank her for having us, though. She bought her a new glass and six bottles of Mackeson.

But when we left, we heard the old woman mutter "Good riddance.."

I was at last in long trousers, and 12 years old. Perhaps we'd surrendered to fate; the hunt was done. It was the perfect time for some domestic stability. And we'd have it – but not for ever.

❖ ❖ ❖ ❖

12: BRIGITTE, JAYNE & CHUCK

> 'It takes time to wear away attachment to old customs, habits, and superstitions. They cannot be got rid of in a day...'
>
> **Hole-in-the-Day** *Ojibway.*

Hessle Road. Oh, how I loved it. Sure enough, I kept faith with Crazy Horse, thought about him every day, but there was so much more to life now. Hessle Road, like the Sioux; a nation unto itself. It had everything. Fish was our buffalo. Ten minutes one way and you'd be on the docks, with all their exotic excitement. There were probably sixty pubs along Hessle Road, all doing a roaring trade. There was the fabulous, cavernous 2,000 seater Langham cinema, and not far past that the old and pokey, yet curiously inviting Eureka Picture House, with its elaborate cream stone Edwardian façade. There were probably a dozen excellent fish and chip shops where the cod and haddock came in straight from St. Andrew's Dock. And opposite Constable Street stood Hessle Road's own last chance saloon, the Oyster Bar, a place where they sold coffee, tea, hot dogs – but no oysters. On the corner of Constable Street stood the brilliant emporium of the poor and down-hearted, Boyes, a massive shop where the clothes and footwear were cheap, sometimes stylish, and the customers cheaper.

And one thing merchant navy men and fishermen do at sea is read. This meant that Hessle Road had a number of pulp book shops selling every second hand work one could think of, as well as having fabulous comic sections. I soon began reading the works of science fiction writers like Ray Bradbury, Isaac Asimov and Robert Sheckley. They were even better than Dan Dare. In fact most of my pocket money went on second hand paperbacks. There was Madeley Street baths, where you could use water, hot or cold, in three ways; swimming, a hot slipper bath, or take your weekly washing in a pram to the wash-house.

The memories of our previous privations began to fade. The house on Boynton Street had three bedrooms, a dining room and a special, hardly-to-be-used front room. It had no bathroom, but a large back yard with outside toilet. But it had electricity, gas, and a kitchen sink with a tap! Now I had my own room at last, the back bedroom. Mam and Dad had the middle bedroom, and Patrick and Alexander the front.

With plenty of construction work Dad was doing better, and we didn't get behind with the rent. Mam got a part time job at Riley High School on the Boulevard. One of the first things Dad bought once we'd settled in was a brand new Stella radio set. This humming, Bakelite-cased valve-driven masterpiece picked up Luxembourg a treat, and if I got up early enough in the morning, I could fiddle with the dial and find music which made the hair stand up on the back of my pink neck. The American Forces Network station, (AFN) based somewhere in Germany, faded away with the sunrise, but in the early hours of dawn darkness, they played songs which were in the American charts, and there were things happening across the pond which filled me with joy. Louis Jordan, Fats Domino, and one day, I heard Little Richard. When would this all come to dreary Britain?

Eventually, the time came to decide whether I would stay at Somerset Street School or move on to some form of higher education. My true desire was to attend some kind of art school. I'd become reasonable at drawing and had dabbled in watercolours, and what I'd read about the disparate, wild lives of the great artists appealed immensely. But when I mentioned the possibility of an art career, Dad went ballistic.

"What?! Poncing around in a smock and beret and living in an attic with a prostitute?"

I particularly liked the second half of his question. I supposed that to pay the prostitute I would have to sell my paintings, but that was OK by me. But he went on.

"You could join the bloody army – that'd do you good."

Mam thankfully stepped into the breach.

"Oh, aye, look what good it's done you."

"But he can't be a bloody *artist*!" exclaimed Dad.

Sadly, Mam veered over to his camp.

"No. I'll tell you what, son; all my family's been to sea. It's a good life, you'll see the world, you won't have to shoot anyone or kill foreigners, and the food's good. I think you'd do well at a nautical school."

I had seen the inmates of Hull's Nautical School in their square-rig uniforms every day, because I passed along the Boulevard where the school was based en route to Somerset Street. Yet the entire crème de la crème of future Hull sailors did not study their navigation at the Boulevard. They went to the nautical establishment to end all nautical establishments, Hull's Trinity House Navigation School. It was so nautical it was actually on a dockside – and still is. There were two entry levels to Trinity House. I'm not sure how it worked, yet there existed a kind of class system where the better-off lad, from a more middle class background, had some way in above the rest of us, the scholarship boys. Because of their more elevated status, they did not have to wear the odd 19th century Nelsonian uniform, but were allowed to dress in the more familiar square-rig of the modern Merchant Navy officer. We, the scholarship boys, were the rough end of the admissions system and had to take an entrance exam.

Mam and Dad insisted, with the encouragement of Mam's brother, the sea-going Uncle Laurie, that I should look at the career of a Merchant Navy officer and take the Trinity House examination. So my fanciful dreams of being a free-wheeling artist who wrote short stories as a sideline were crushed. Once again I thought of Crazy Horse and his band, their dreams of being left alone to live the life of their choice in the Black Hills had been exchanged for the formality of giving in to the U.S. government and placing themselves at the mercy of the Indian Agency. Little did the Sioux realise even in 1877 that their capitulation would lead ultimately to the destruction of their very culture, even to the banning of their native language.

Despite my appalling lack of mathematical skill, I managed to pass the exam. I deliberately didn't try hard enough, hoping that failure would change the course of my life and I could do something more romantic. However, once I realised that early in 1957 I would indeed be starting at Trinity House, I attempted a positive re-evaluation. It did at least lead to a career on the ocean wave, and the chance to see all manner of exotic locations. I had little choice but to approach the project with forced enthusiasm and give it a try.

Yet there would be the final months of my time at good old Somerset Street to enjoy. One event that autumn was memorable. There was a tough guy in our class called Al Novis. His brothers were at sea on trawlers, and like some other lads in the class he had a penchant for brawling in the school yard. There were always fights among fishermen in Hull. In pubs, outside pubs, in the gutter, every night was one of blood, snot and ambulances.

The only sport I was involved in at Somerset Street was the game of rounders. I liked it because it seemed vaguely American and reminiscent of baseball. We would travel on the bus to play, to a sports field near Hessle. One day, when I was swinging my rounders bat, I missed a shot and Al Novis began shouting abuse at me, and obviously trying to start a fight. I was no good at fighting, and hated being bullied, but once he'd pushed me to the ground and kicked me, something in me snapped. I picked up the bat, got to my feet and chased him all around the field, landing a blow on him whenever he was in reach. Our teacher, Mick Brown, could see the terror I was inflicting on my attacker and was shouting across the grass "Bainton! Stop it! Stop that *now!*" It was the one occasion at Somerset Street when, in tandem with Al Novis, I got six of the best from Mr. Brown's cane. Yet it was worth it. Al Novis never bullied me again and we became friends, even swapping cigarette cards. Then one day he told me that his two older brothers were home from sea for a week and they were taking him camping to a wooded area past Hessle along the banks of the Humber known as Little Switzerland. He asked if I would like to come along for a weekend under canvas. As the Bilton Grange Wolf Cubs had never sent for me, this was an opportunity I was not going to miss.

This invitation coincided nicely with a nefarious little act I'd pulled off, courtesy of Radio Luxembourg. One of their music shows was sponsored by Wincarnis Tonic Wine. If you sent a self-addressed post card to a London box number, then you'd receive a free sample bottle of this mysterious beverage. In those days the morning post came often before 8 am, and I waited every day until a couple of days before the camping trip, my package arrived. I was pleased with this surreptitious success, because I'd already come a cropper with another Radio Luxembourg free offer. I didn't know then who Humphrey Lytleton was, but he was to be the star at something called the Hornsey Jazz Festival, and there were a number of free tickets going. Naturally, I'd imagined it to be Hornsea, the local site of our infamous cattle wagon experience. Sadly my attendance was not an option – I didn't know there was a 'Hornsey' somewhere in London. Then again, a free bottle of proper pick-me-up made up for a lack of jazz trumpet. I hid my clandestine booze upstairs under my bed. I was both relieved and surprised that Mam and Dad agreed to my weekend in the wild with the Novis clan.

On the Friday night I was amazed when a taxi came for

me. Crammed in the back was Al and his brothers. I can't remember their names, but they were young fishermen, probably still in their late teens or early twenties. When you're as young as I was then, anyone over 15 seems ancient. I think they were both deckie learners, a rank in trawling something equivalent to a junior deckhand. I shouldn't have been surprised by the taxi, because looking back, fishermen, known to all on Hessle Road when they paid off as the 'three day millionaires', seemed to travel everywhere by cab, with the older hands and the skippers and mates often hiring a taxi for a full day's pub-crawling.

Apart from my wellies and a gabardine raincoat, I wasn't exactly kitted out for the bivouac experience. I had a carrier bag with a towel, a clean vest and underpants, toothbrush, soap and a towel, and Mam had packed me two Fletcher's pork pies. I had hidden my Wincarnis inside my mac, and although it produced a suspicious looking lump, no-one said anything.

It was still light when the tents were set up. I'd imagined we would all be in one tent, but the big hearted lads had brought two. We were in the middle of a field, hemmed in by the tall outcrop of Little Switzerland to the north and hedges on the other three sides. A fire was lit and we sat around eating sausages and beans. All my Sioux feelings flooded back. This was as good as it got. Suddenly I was Crazy Horse again. All that was missing was a promise of a buffalo hunt.

After we'd cleaned the plates in water from a nearby ditch, the two big lads announced that they were going to the pub, and as it was almost dark, that we two youngsters should retire to out tent. We had no sleeping bags, but some decent ex-army blankets, and we decided not to get undressed.

Lying there in the dark with the lad who had once been my nemesis was an odd feeling. We talked about school, films and radio, and then I decided it was time to produce my contraband. The darkness and the silence punctuated only now and then by forlorn ship's whistles out on the nearby

Humber, made us feel like true adventurers. Even more so when we lit a candle in a jam jar and I uncorked the Wincarnis.

"What's that, then?" asked Al, staring at the bottle.

"Booze," I said.

"What – like Rum?"

"I don't know. Never had any rum."

I took a swig from the bottle. It was an odd, heady, herby taste and as it went down my untested gullet, it left a warm, pleasant feeling. I suppose, knowing what I know now, that this first taste of evil alcohol was probably a bit more than my system could handle. According to an on-line outfit known as The Whisky Exchange, the product is described thus:

> 'Wincarnis Tonic Wine is a blend of enriched wine and malt extract infused with a bewildering variety of botanicals including gentian root, mugwort, angelica root, balm mint, fennel seed, coriander seed, peppermint leaves, cardamom seeds and cassia bark. A classier alternative to Buckfast'.

That's more than a wine; it's a Neanderthal salad. Not only that, but it packs a hefty 14% alcohol content.

I passed the bottle to Al. He guzzled for a few seconds then smacked his lips and passed it back.

"Wossit mean?" he slurred.

"Wasswot mean?" I slurred back.

"Win... Winc-arnis?"

I gulped more down.

"I dunno. Tastes good, though."

Twenty minutes later, after we'd drained the bottle, we were crawling through the tent flap and gazing blearily up at the twinkling stars.

"Gorrany more?" asked Al.

"Nope. S'all gone."

The stars began to spin and swirl. Al started laughing and I

followed. We felt stupid but strangely warm and utterly carefree. I wondered if the two older lads were drinking Wincarnis in the pub. If so, they must be feeling great, too.
The euphoria, however, began to fade and was replaced by an odd kind of queasiness. Eventually, we crawled back into the tent and, incapable of any intelligible conversation, lay back in our blankets and fell into something approaching a coma.

I don't know what time it was (watches were a luxury then) but it was pitch black and Al was prodding me in the ribs.
I sat up, blinking, yet it was still too black to see anything.
"What?"
"Lissen..." whispered Al.
I listened; I could hear snoring from the other tent, so the lads must have returned long before from the pub.
"Snoring," I said, yawning. My mouth felt like the inside of a wrestler's jock strap and my head was spinning.
"Naw ..." whispered Al again ... *"listen..."*
Then I heard it. There was something heavy, something breathing, and something out there in the dark with only a barrier of War Department canvas separating us from it. I froze.
"What is it?"
"Fucked if I know!" hissed Al. I was taken aback by his language, as I'd not really learned to swear properly yet.
Then there was a thumping noise, and it vibrated through the ground beneath our blankets and suddenly, the tent collapsed on us. From the outside, I suppose our ensuing panic would have fitted in well in a Three Stooges movie. Two shuddering, canvas-covered humps leaping around in the dark. We were on our feet, yelling in terror, totally covered by the collapsed tent, staggering, tripping, feeling for the opening. When we found it, the moon had risen, and standing in front of us was a large brown cow. Behind the cow, clad in their underpants and waving torches, were Al's brothers.

The cow gave a mighty 'Mooo!' then ambled off.

When I finally got home to Boynton Street after our camping interlude, I still had traces of a hangover. Yet I had found the Wincarnis experience interesting. I wondered if beer had similar effects. Sadly, it would be some time before I found out.

Before we broke up for holidays I had managed to earn some extra cash to supplement my half crown per week pocket money. I had answered a post card advert in a newsagent's window in Division Road for a paper lad.

Leaving Somerset Street for the last time was a sad event. I had made good friends there and I was the only sucker going to Trinity House. Everyone else seemed to be destined for a career on trawlers.

I became quite skilled at delivering papers. The *Hull Daily Mail* had a healthy circulation and my round included the area from West Dock Avenue through to Gillette Street. This was seven streets, with terraces, and I had to make sure that I batched all the papers in sequence and could run around fast enough to complete the job in less than two hours. The wage, paid every Friday night, was six shillings and nine pence. (About .35p in new money). Added to my regular two shillings and sixpence this gave me the luxurious sum of almost ten bob to do with as I wished. I would hang on to that job for the next year and a half.

One of my new fascinations was sex. I'd not yet indulged in this much-vaunted physical activity, but through the good offices of such publications as *Spick and Span*, the nigh-on illicit bare-breasted, stocking topped photography of Harrison Marks and a weekly dose of lingerie glamour in *The Reveille, a* saucy stable mate of *The Daily Mirror*, I had at least formed a healthy interest in female anatomy. Well ... *some* would say healthy. However, I did not develop hairs on my palms nor did I go blind, contrary to the warnings given out by various uncles. I can't remember quite when, but during this pervy period of physical awakening, the *Reveille* published a series of life-size centre-fold pull-outs of Brigitte Bardot, high-heeled and clad, as I recall, in a white basque, looking cheekily back at her many admirers of her velvety shoulder. The first week was her lower legs and dainty feet, the second probably thighs to waist, then came the upper torso followed by the head. According to some nostalgia experts, when all four sections were assembled, it fell short of being 'life sized' as it measured just over four feet, when Brigitte, we believed, was around five feet four. But what the hell! A near life sized beautiful *French* woman in her underwear on your bedroom wall? She was even sexier than Alma Cogan! I have since discovered that at the same time I was assembling my private Brigitte in Hull, across country John Lennon, then at Liverpool's Quarry Bank School, was doing the same.

Which brings us on to music. My early morning trawls through the airwaves of Europe in the direction of American Forces Network had set my soul on fire. I had experienced two songs, *Roll Over Beethoven* and *Too Much Monkey Business* by some wild vocalist and guitar wizard called Chuck Berry. I had no time for Bill Haley and his Comets, but Elvis had arrived on the scene and I wanted more than anything to be closer to the music. Rock and Roll and sex; it was a potent combination, yet it still felt slightly out of reach, as if I was the kid looking in the sweetshop window.

I started at Trinity House School in the spring term of 1957. But before that utter change in my life, I had spent my Saturdays with a Somerset Street school friend called Dave Hollingsworth – because he had the most desirable device in the world – a record player. We only had perhaps six clunky 78 rpm discs, but they were terrific. We'd discovered Lonnie Donegan, Little Richard, Elvis, Jerry Lee Lewis and the Everly Brothers. With my accumulated paper round earnings and pocket money I had managed to buy a florid, ridiculous red and black striped shirt from Boyes store on Hessle Road. I made myself a bootlace tie – from a real bootlace. I also had some fluorescent socks – 2 pairs, in yellow and red. I envied Dave Hollingsworth, whose parents were slightly better off, because he had some tight black drainpipe pants and a fleck jacket with a velvet collar. But I was determined to be my own cool cat. I bought some velvet and sewed it onto my school jacket, and I sat up one night stitching up the lower legs of my trousers so that when I put them on the next day I looked a like a ballet dancer in jodhpurs. Yet me and Dave were cool. We'd both lusted after Brigitte Bardot, but one night at the Langham cinema proved that there were even greater magnets of teen lust. *The Girl Can't Help It* was a movie with everything. Gene Vincent, Eddie Cochran, Little Richard ... and Jayne Mansfield. In the heady, organic days before silicone, there were few women as outstandingly pneumatic – and as pretty – as Miss Mansfield. Diana Dors and Anita Ekberg were fine, but no substitute.

I felt snappy and happy in my Teddy Boy coolness until one day, just before I was due to start at Trinity House, I decided to return to Somerset Street to say a proper goodbye to my mates and teachers. Their term had started a week before my new school's, and I thought it would be groovy to pay the old place a visit as a 'civilian'. It was, after all, to be the last chance I might have of cultural self expression before the two years of quasi-military discipline which lay ahead.

After dinner one day I donned my florid rock'n'roll outfit and ambled along to Somerset Street. My ex-classmates seemed reasonably impressed, but it was when I paid a visit to the study of the headmaster, Mr. Hannah, that I had to pause for a re-think. I knocked on his door.

"Enter!" came the voice. I went in. Mr. Hannah was sitting behind his big oak desk inspecting registers. He looked up.

"Ah. Bainton, is it?"

"Yes, sir. Just come to say thank you and that I'll be starting at Trinity House next week."

He was looking me up and down in a curious way.

"I see. Is there a circus in town?"

"Er ... I don't think so, sir. Why?"

He threw his head back and gave a dry little chuckle.

"Oh, well, I was thinking perhaps you'd joined one. I was admiring your clown's outfit."

I felt vaguely insulted, but he did leave his desk, shake my hand and wish me well. A clown? Me?

The clowning, however, was about to come to an abrupt end.

❖ ❖ ❖ ❖

13: BULL, BRASS & BLANCO

'I seen that great warrior before we split off by ourselves; he had a face full of sharpened edges, wore no ornamentation whatever, no paint, no feathers; he was like a living weapon.'

Thomas Berger, *Little Big Man* (novel) 1964

After my formative years spent wearing my other clown's outfits of makeshift ex-government clothing, plimsolls and wellingtons, the superb uniform we were given for Trinity House was a pleasure to wear. I'd no longer be regarded as a walking peculiarity, a cross between a Desert Rat and a defrocked admiral, because at this new school, at least the great majority of us would dress the same.

The uniform had been collected a few weeks before term began after a measuring-up session at P. R. Davies, the tailors under Hull's City Hall. It was quality throughout. The jacket was what was commonly referred to in Nelson's day as a 'bumfreezer' (it ended just above your buttocks) with two rows of brass buttons and two pockets. It had a stiff white canvas collar with two brass buttons. These were removable, so that the collar could be frequently whitened using Blanco. This was a product originally made from pipe clay by Joseph Pickering & Co. in Sheffield. (After 185 years they went into receivership as I was writing this). Blanco, supplied to the armed forces of 60 countries around the globe, came in a round block, to which you added a little water. Of course, the Army had been using Blanco for years for their belts, so this additional bit of bull routine, designed to steal yet another half hour of your precious time, fitted well as an extra discipline for a bunch of potential lounge lizards and would-be Teddy Boys. There was also a nice waistcoat, with more brass buttons, and the whole ensemble, including the trousers, was made of the finest dark navy moleskin material. As well as a peaked cap, bearing the school's badge (with a removable white cover for the summer terms) there was a white waistcoat and white canvas trousers for church parades and founder's days. Completing all this were blue striped shirts with detachable collars, black ties, and smart black leather shoes. I have to admit, that first day in 1957 when I put this outfit on, I felt pretty damn good.

Before I left home Mam stood back from me and looked me up and down with pride and a tear in her eye.

"You look like a real ship's officer. You're going to be somebody one day."

I already thought I was 'somebody' but that first morning in the Trinity House yard I realised I was nobody. In a similar manner to public school, each class was split into 'houses', although we were known as 'Port Watch' and 'Starboard Watch'. New boys were immediately berated by the older hands as 'fags'. Each watch had its prefect, known as the watch officer. Above this were the school's overall senior officers, from the ranks of the final year big lads, and in charge of the whole hierarchy was the head boy known as the School Captain.

The first thing we learned that morning was that we would be shouted and bellowed at on as many occasions as possible. We had to learn about how to stand at attention, how to stand at ease, how to put distance between ourselves at arm's length when the officer shouted 'right ... dress!' We marched everywhere, but nothing was as peculiar as morning inspection. We would line up in ranks, form by form, in the yard, and the School Captain and a form master would walk along the ranks looking for sartorial slackness. As we were expected to wear button-up braces on our trousers, and not belts (which were apparently the trouser furniture of Satan), we would line up for inspection with our jackets and waistcoats un-buttoned. First our shoes and the crease in our pants got the once-over, then we did the bizarre 'how's your braces' pirouette. This involved first holding your jacket and waistcoat wide open, in the fashion of some adolescent flasher, then once it became established that your braces were on at the front; you did a sharp about turn, a slight sexy bend, and lifted your jacket at the rear so that those all-important braces were attached at the back, too. I found the whole procedure hilarious, yet one unfastened button, one loose collar stud, and you soon lost your sense of humour.

In the somewhat doomy school hall, with its highly polished, ancient ship's bell, we were lectured on what was expected of us by the Headmaster, Mr. Eddon, known to all as 'Charlie'. He had a slightly high-pitched voice with the residue of a Scottish burr, and when speaking about school dinners referred to food as 'Fudd.' He had a hawk-eyed secretary named Miss Bird, who the older hands warned us about – apparently, she could be trouble. The other teachers were a mixed bunch of mainly ex-military disciplinarians. Science and Physics came via Mr. Richardson, who reminded us of a less hirsute Jimmy 'Whacko' Edwards. His nickname, oddly, was 'Kite'. Maths and Navigation, and some seamanship were the province of a somewhat sarcastic Scot, Mr. Campbell, a.k.a. 'Jock'. He was to be my nemesis. PE and more seamanship was the department of a man with the same name, although no relation, to my previous headmaster, Hannah. He was an ex-naval fitness instructor but, unlike some of the other masters, firm and fair and operated lower down on the sadism scale. The oldest and most peculiar member of staff, Mr. Stenner, taught history. Or, to be more accurate, just one bit of history – Dane's Dyke. He was probably at least into his 70s. He travelled on the train every day to Hull from Bridlington. An ex naval petty officer, I believe, he had a fund of nautical stories yet only accessed around 5% of them. When not talking about Dane's Dyke, (a Bronze Age bank and ditch West of Flamborough Head, East Yorkshire), he would usually regale us, chewing on his smelly briar pipe, with the story of the old sailing ship's figurehead he apparently had parked by his front gate at home.

"Aye ... when people come to the house in the dark or the fog, they see this bare-chested damsel and they quake with fear..."

It became such a regular yarn that we all knew it off word perfect.

I soon got used to the spit and polish militaristic world of Trinity House. I had some good classmates, and 1957 really was the year that rock'n'roll stormed the *New Musical Express* charts. Before morning parades we could gather by the gymnasium windows and discuss the records played the previous night on Radio Luxembourg, and I was now a regular early-riser with Mam at 5.30 am so I was ahead of the game by tuning in to AFN. I warned everyone to expect the arrival of a certain Buddy Holly and The Crickets weeks before *That'll Be The Day* hit the UK charts.

But I still yearned for a record player, and in this new teenage company, I knew it would seem childish to bring up the subject of Crazy Horse. Wednesdays were Chapel days when we wore out whites and attended a service in the school's fine chapel, overseen by the rigorous, unsympathetic Reverend Dann. When I told Mam about how this 'Good Christian' seemed to enjoy dropping some poor hapless classmates in it for some minor transgression or other, she said

"I'm not surprised. He was a bit of a squealer when he was a kid." I asked her what she meant.

"We all lived in the same row of houses on Hedon Road when I was a girl. He lived at one side of us, and David Whitfield lived at the other. I don't know what was worse - 'Holy Charlie' Dann or titchy Whitfield singing his head off on a box in the back yard."

Every third Sunday we had to dress in our full whites again for church parade and attend Holy Trinity Church in the Market Place. The whole school would march from our yard in columns three abreast, and in some ways we got a buzz from this. People out for a Sunday stroll would line the pavements on Whitefriargate and they often included teenage girls, and as the saying goes, most girls love a uniform. (Not that we ever 'pulled', though.) The services, with their standard hymns and droning psalms were the tedious part of the day, but by 1 pm we were usually on the way home again.

1957 was a good year. To begin with, for the time being at least, Dad had abandoned his 'way out west' pioneering fixation and was in steady building work. Mam had her morning cleaning job. Patrick was at nursery school, Alexander at juniors, and although we still had no bathroom or indoor toilet, we had something more important – not long after my 14th birthday we got our first television set. Now I could watch the only TV show worth watching – *The 6-5 Special*. It became possible to see what Lonnie Donegan actually looked like in the flesh. Of course, we had to put up with rubbish such as Don Lang and his Frantic Five, the wheedling tones of Russ Hamilton and the chirpy, 'Cockenee' ersatz rock and roll of Tommy Steele. But in the main it was guys with guitars, with no sign of the BBC's Emperors of musical boredom, Billy Cotton, Henry Hall, Edmundo Ross or Victor Sylvester at all. Suddenly, we were not little clones of your wartime fathers – we were something new called 'teenagers' with our own music and culture.

Christmas 1957 knocked the socks off any yuletide which had gone before. We had actually got used once again to living in the same house for an unprecedented period of stability. We had electricity, gas and water. We even got a piano! Mam had reached her Grade 6 in piano as a girl, and on Sunday nights she'd go with us into the forbidden enclave of the front room and play us selections of music. On Saturdays Mam would send me to music lessons in Hessle to an absolute martinet of a woman, a dry, monochrome aggressive German spinster of such ferocity that I believe she was expelled from the SS for cruelty. I tried learning the piano, oh, how I tried. But I wanted a guitar. Sadly, I wanted a record player even more.

Around late November that year Mam had gone to work one morning and, passing her open bedroom door, I noticed a large cardboard package on top of her wardrobe. Curious, I stood on a chair and lifted the loose cardboard lid. My heart soared to high heaven. Nestling in the box was a green and white leatherette-clad record player. I lifted its lid and breathed in the vital odour of its Collaro 10-record changer deck and black rubber turntable mat. I knew by this time that Santa was a figment of our imagination, but I was more than impressed with the seasonal love this represented.

That Christmas morning was the open gateway to my passion for music. The record player stood on the table in the front room by the window. Mam had made a roaring fire, and the forbidden inner sanctum seemed totally hospitable for a change. Added to my ecstasy was the fact that my gift had come, courtesy of yet another club cheque from Uncle Ken, our friendly loan shark, complete with a selection of ten of the top chart records of December 1957. The first 78 rpm disc, on the Coral label, I placed carefully on the deck was Jackie Wilson's vibrant, bouncy *Reet Petite*. It remains as thrilling today as it did then. Not all the records met with my approval, but I kept quiet, naturally; Mam and Dad had obviously gone to great trouble and expense and I knew it.

The other 9 records were: (in descending order of approval)

Buddy Holly & The Crickets *That'll Be The Day*
Jerry Lee Lewis *Great Balls of Fire*
The Everly Brothers *Wake Up Little Susie*
Little Richard *Keep A-knockin'*
Elvis Presley *Santa Bring My Baby Back To Me*
Lonnie Donegan *My Dixie Darling*

Gracie Fields; (!!) *Mary's Boy Child*
Paul Anka *Diana*
Russ Hamilton *We Will Make Love.*

The last three in the list were particularly obnoxious. I could have lived with Harry Belafonte's original *Mary's Boy Child*, but Gracie Fields? I could never see her appeal. I couldn't stand Paul Anka, and Russ Hamilton's record had been a hit earlier in the year and his wheedling, insipid vocals on his drippy ballad seemed about as relevant to rock and roll as I was to mathematics. But *what* a Christmas present. I now knew that with the money from my paper round I could afford to buy a new record every week – they cost around 6/3d per single at the time. I could work my way through the charts with ease.

After a hearty breakfast of pork pie and dandelion and burdock, I played the top seven of my records around three times each. I can't recall what presents Alexander or Patrick got that day, but I did get the impression that they were both slightly jealous of the way their big brother had prospered. Sadly, my suspicions would be borne out in a dramatic fashion later in the day.

We had our Christmas dinner at 2 pm. Even this was special, because we had a roast chicken. It was the most delicious thing I had ever tasted, apart from cinder toffee and coconut ice. Patrick was five years old and a mischievous mite, just like his brother Alexander. They were a real handful at that time. As Patrick didn't like Christmas pudding, he asked to leave the table to play with his new toys in the front room.

About half an hour after we'd pulled our last crackers, I could smell something scorching or burning. I went into the front room, and the sight before me almost made me faint with horror. The lid of the record player was open, and blue smoke was billowing out. I ran over to my dream machine and looked in. Patrick had taken the shovel from the fireside companion set and heaped three mounds of smouldering ash from the fire grate into the record player.

I yelled at the top of my voice. Dad came running in, grabbed the smoking machine and ran with it into the back yard, turned it upside down and shook it vigorously, the still glowing ash and embers scattering on the flagstones. Mam came out with a dustpan and brush, cleaned out the record player then swept the yard.

Back in the front room we examined the damage. I was in deep despair. The leatherette covering the record player's case had blistered here and there, and parts of the rubber turntable mat had melted. The were burn marks on the lovely cream Collaro arm. My greatest concern was – would it still work? I put the Jackie Wilson on and everything seemed to function. That record player served me well for many years, and when Alexander went to live in Finland in 1982, apparently it went with him. As far as I know, it may still be in use. The odd thing about how faulty our memories can be is that for years after the ash-on-the-turntable incident, I blamed Alexander for the crime. It was only half a century later that Patrick owned up – or, at least, reminded me – that he was the kid with the shovel.

1958 was looking good. At first. I was still meeting my old mate Dave Hollingsworth on some Saturdays because he now possessed something I would still have to wait a whole year for – a guitar. Neither of us knew how to tune it, or how to play the damned thing, but we would spend Saturday afternoons posing and miming to Lonnie Donegan records. I tried to make my own guitar using a fish box and a length of old banister rail, but it didn't work. Worse than that, it stank to high heaven. Yet with my paper round wages and now my increased pocket money of 5/- (.25p) most Saturdays were a sheer delight. After my piano lessons with Frau *Ober gruppenfuhrer* Himmler at Hessle in the mornings, (which were going absolutely nowhere) Mam would send me to a friendly butcher called Ted (I can't recall his surname) who had a shop opposite Madeley Street on Hessle Road. Ted's sausages, at 1/- per pound, were gorgeous. I would arrive home just before noon with three pounds of Ted's brilliant bangers, and Mam would be baking fresh bread. She would put the sausages into a roasting tin with chopped onions into the oven, and once they'd cooked to a crisp brown, transfer the tin to the top of the stove, add two tins of tomatoes and make a gravy with Burdall's Gravy Salt. Saturday lunch at 1 pm was my favourite; the hot bread, the sausages, that gravy. No vegetables; no potatoes; just sausages, onion and tomato gravy and bread. Then it was into the best Teddy Boy togs I could muster and off into town with mates from school to buy records from Sydney Scarborough's cavernous music shop under the city hall. Scarborough's was great because they had a bank of listening booths. I suppose it was an example of 'try before you buy' but we just went to the counter, told them what discs we wanted to listen to, all cram into a booth and make our decisions. It was a simple thrill – the best kind there is. I would have to be back at the newsagents on Division Road by 4pm to complete my paper round, then after tea, just before 7 pm, we'd all crowd onto the trolley bus again to go to the pictures.

There was one cinema on George Street in Hull called the Curzon, where they specialised in what Mam called 'mucky pictures'. I can't recall the titles – they were obscure movies even then, but they promised a slight touch of exotica in the form of a revealed stocking top or, if you were particularly lucky – a nipple. The films were often French with sub titles, and we didn't give a hoot for the plot; they just had a dark, beckoning adult atmosphere which left us realising how much growing up we still had to do. Gaining admission, though, was by no means guaranteed. These were 'X' rated movies and to watch them you had to be 16. It all depended on how busy the queue was at the box office and who was on duty behind the glass. We didn't look 16, that's a fact.

But sometimes the lie worked. Other Saturdays it didn't, so we would end up seeing something across the street at the Dorchester or further along at the Criterion.

By Spring 1958 my Uncle Charlie's comment on my unsuitability to be one of Crazy Horse's band had a new interpretation; I realised that I could never be a Merchant Navy navigating officer as long as, (to paraphrase Charlie) 'I had a hole in my arse'. Trinity House, with its daily grind of snapping to attention, saluting, inspections, and marching everywhere, was beginning to feel like a cultural cul-de-sac. I was good enough at seamanship; I could splice a rope, do the knots, and fared well in our weekly lifeboat rowing practice in the old Victoria Dock. I shone at English and art, and was an expert on Dane's Dyke. But the maths, oh, Lord, *the maths*. Tangents, cosines, logarithms. I was like a deaf Welshman trying to speak Cantonese. That said, I wasn't the only square peg in Trinity House's numerous round holes. There were plenty of Dumbos like me.

I recall one lad, named Potter, ostensibly forced into this establishment by his parents, who hated and loathed every day he spent on Princes Dock Side. I realised where I might be heading one day when our maths and navigation supremo, Jock Campbell, made Potter stand on his chair to give us the answer to some algebraic brain-twister on the blackboard. To people like me and Potter, the chalk marks may as well have been in ancient Greek. As Jock launched into a tirade of sarcasm against the befuddled Potter, standing on his chair like some medieval occupant of the town stocks, the lad suddenly went red in the face and cracked. I can't recall the full explosive narrative, but it went something like

"Fuck you! Fuck your school, fuck your algebra, I don't know the answer and I can't do it! Fuck your merchant navy and your ships!"

This resulted in Potter being forcibly removed from his reluctant perch and instructed to go to the headmaster's office. Instead, he went to the cloakroom, collected his raincoat and went home. He didn't last long at the school after that, and although I couldn't have predicted it at the time, I would not be far behind him. In some ways I knew I was letting my parents, and my Mam's seafaring brothers, down. No matter what I thought of it, the fact was that Trinity House was a fine establishment if, as a pupil, you could hack it. It turned out some of the most excellent officers and captains and many old hands were proud to be known by the school's sobriquet, (as it applied to our uniform) as 'white-arsed terriers'. Could I have tried harder? Perhaps not. Some people can't dance or hold a tune. They couldn't be opera singers or Fred Astaire. I was not going to make it to Starbuck or Captain Ahab status; I was forever doomed to be Ishmael. I was the beneficiary of an education, though, which was as good as any High school's in the city. Art College would have been better, but despite my abject failure to adapt to its laudable traditions, I do not regret my time as a Trinity House cadet.

What there was to regret in the summer of 1958 was the sudden return of Dad's rural pioneering desires. The horror re-surfaced one hot night. I was sitting in my back bedroom looking through the window. From this vantage point I could easily see into next door's back yard, where our neighbour, Mr. Cosley, would frequent her outside loo and always leave the door wide open. She was a portly woman in her early 50s, always in curlers and a floral pinny, and she cared not a jot as she sat there, smoking a fag, with her frock and pinny around her waist, varicosed legs apart, capacious bloomers around her ample ankles. For all I know she was probably aware of my presence at the window, but this sexless, indiscrete display of mature womanhood fascinated me. A boy never thinks of his own mother in any other way; your Mam was simply your Mam; her age was always indistinct, her womanhood an unfathomable mystery. But seeing other grown-up women in the way I saw Mrs. Cosley made me think deeply about the opposite sex. I would look at her on the toilet, then glance back at my bedroom wall at Jayne and Brigitte. Had she ever looked anything remotely like that? Was this what girls turned into? Now, fifty plus years on, I realise that the same conundrum applied equally to the male of the species. I could never have realised back then, as a fit, spritely ten stone teenager, with no sartorial size problems, that one day I'd end up as a florid tub of lard who would be frequently on the verge of tears as he searches the racks in Tesco's clothing section, only to realise that he is no longer part of the market for jeans, and that they don't do a waist 46 in anything other than jogging pants.

As I sat there watching Mrs. Cosley pull her voluminous knickers up, Mam's voice snapped me into attention.

"Stop that! That's a bad thing – you shouldn't be looking!"

I moved away from the window. It was almost dark and she switched my bedroom light on.

"I've got some news."

"Oh ... what's that, then?"

"We're moving."

My heart sank like an anvil tossed into the dock.

"Oh..." I sighed, "but *why*?"

"Your Dad and I don't like Hessle Road all that much. I can't stand the smell of fish any more. We need some fresh air out in the country."

Dark thoughts of Mytholmroyd loomed.

"Oh, Mam – not another cottage? Not somewhere with no electric again – what about my record player?"

She shook her head and sighed as she sat down on the edge of the bed.

"No, no, we learned our lesson there. The place we're going has got water and electric, and it's got a massive garden." I remained unimpressed.

"Where is it? Not the other side of the country again?"

"Hedon."

Hedon was a large village we only passed through on the bus or train on the rare occasions we might spend a day at the seaside at Withernsea. I listened in dismay as she told me that the new place had a name – Elm Bank – and it was the last house on an estate of countrified dwellings, mostly smallholdings. She then warned me that I would no longer have my own room, as the three of us lads would have to share one room. Yet Dad had obviously sold her on the chickens and vegetable garden routine yet again. I knew it was futile to argue.

"So ... I'll have to get the bus from Hedon into Hull for school every day."

"It's only half an hour into town."

"What's this place like? What kind of house is it?"

"Well, I went to see it the other day with your Dad. It's a wooden bungalow, with a big shed and a greenhouse. And it's by a row of trees by big open fields. You'll love it. It's just the place for Crazy Horse."

Tsunke Witco, my Achilles heel. I felt slightly outraged that the chief should crop up as part of a bit of estate agency-type persuasive patter. I hadn't thought of Crazy Horse for a while, but now he rode angrily through my mind again. He must have felt like this when, with his band starving and down-hearted in the January of 1877, General Crook's aides rode out to promise him food and security on the reservation providing he vacated his beloved Black Hills. Like me, he had little choice.

"When are we going?"

"August. But before we go, we're going to all have a nice holiday – a day in Cleethorpes."

Oh, I thought. *Whoopie-bleedin' doo*! A day in Cleethorpes. Not a week or a weekend, but a day. To be followed by what? More rural drudgery? More nasty farmers? I could hardly believe what I was hearing.

❖ ❖ ❖ ❖

Crazy Horse and The Coalman

14: THE CURSE OF UNCLE KEN

*'When Crazy Horse and his people came in sight
of Camp Robinson, the chiefs started
to sing their brave-heart song.
The warriors picked it up and then
the women and children joined in.'*

Judith St. George *Crazy Horse,* Putnams. NY 1994

When Crazy Horse finally gave up his life on the Plains he realised that he could no longer live his life as a free spirit. The greedy white hunters had killed all the buffalo simply for their hides, leaving the skinned corpses – the staple diet of the Sioux, to rot in the sun. They had built the iron railroad through the hunting grounds, soldiers had built forts, and miners were scrabbling for gold on every rock face. The peace and certainty the Sioux had always enjoyed was gone forever.

In some ways, perhaps that's what happens when we make our exit from childhood. The certainties of school, parental care, being fed and clothed suddenly become your own obligations as you stagger into the world of work. Between the ages of 16 to 65 you're on your own, with a burden of responsibility. Of course, that's a facile comparison because its not anywhere near as bad as losing your hunting grounds, your culture, country and your way of life, but for me, as a simple-minded kid, the plight of the Sioux had some resonance.

Moving from the joy and security of Hessle Road to some indistinct new abode in the country felt like my surrender. I

wished that I had indeed been good at maths and navigation, because then I would be guaranteed a place in the Merchant Navy and would finally get away from it all. Now the future was uncertain. So what was there to look forward to?
The unadulterated joy of a day at Cleethorpes.

Towards the end of that summer the problem of clothes and looking cool became much more intense. One Saturday, our school gang had been to see James Dean in *Rebel Without A Cause*. Here was an icon we could aspire to. The T-shirt, the red Harrington jacket, and, above all – those Levi jeans. Someone brought a film magazine to school containing a feature on James Dean and his cool look. We read with interest about these 'jeans' things. Why did they look so groovy? Why did they fit so well? We had nothing like Levis or Wranglers in Britain at that time. But I studied that article and, with a magnifying glass, inspected those jeans as closely as possible. Apparently, according to James Dean, he would buy a new pair of Levis and sit in a bath of cold water patting them to his legs. The ensuing shrinkage, once they'd dried out, was what gave these sublime trousers their perfect fit. I had no idea how, if ever, I was going to get hold of a pair, but somehow I thought I might be able to get an approximation of that 'look' with a little creative adaptation.

As ever, Uncle Ken, our club check/moneylender had kept up his weekly visits. He'd progressed over the years from a pushbike to a moped, and in the late summer of 1958 he surprised us all by arriving one Friday lunchtime in a Ford Popular. He was obviously doing as well as ever. I was ambivalent over his value to the family. In those days only posh folk had bank accounts and cheque books. You didn't get loans from banks at our end of the food chain. Mam had tried it once. It was a hilarious scenario.
She had seen a poster offering loans in the window of the Trustee Savings Bank on the corner of Bond Street and George Street in Hull. She made an appointment.

She duly went along in her worn old coat and headscarf, carrying her tartan shopping bag. Sitting in the manager's office, she felt distinctly uncomfortable. The manager had forms spread out on the desk, and peered at her over his spectacles.

"So ... Mrs – Bainton? I see you would like to borrow £100."

"Yes, if that's OK."

He jotted the figure down and took her address.

"Do you hold an account with us?"

"Oh, yes. I've been with the Trustee Savings Bank for over 30 years." The Manager looked slightly surprised and smiled.

"Ah ... do you have your account details?"

From her shopping bag she produced an oval metal money box with a slot in the top. It was engraved with the words *Trustee Savings Bank*. She rattled it; there was obviously some coinage inside.

"We all got one of these at school when I was a girl. So I've kept mine."

The manager held it in his palm, wearing a slightly puzzled expression.

"And *this* is your account?"

"Yes. Had it all this time. Never drawn anything out."

He rattled the tin.

"And how much is in here?" he asked.

"Oh, probably half a crown," she said, proudly.

Needless to say, she never got her £100. That was Uncle Ken's department.

I knew that the trip to Cleethorpes plus yet another house move would warrant a clothing cheque. Sure enough, that day he'd arrived in his Ford, over his dinner in our kitchen of bubble and squeak and three cups of tea, his big leather money bag and leather-bound account book were soon on the table. Mam got a £30 cheque to spend on clothes for the family. I sat there wondering if this bloke had any conscience at all. OK, without him I would have had no record player, and we would have been in short supply of wellingtons, underwear and plimsolls. But with his soaring interest rates, and, as we knew, in many cases, where people were in arrears, he'd sent the bailiffs in, how did this parasite sleep at nights? And why did he earn the title 'Uncle', and why did we feed the bugger? These were the angry sparks which would later ignite my passion for left wing politics.

The next day, a sunny, warm Saturday, Mam left Patrick and Alexander at home with Dad and together, we were bound for Shields's Army Stores on Hessle Road. As regulars there, at least two or three times per year, Mrs. and Mrs. Shields knew us well. Their real name, apparently, was Schultz. I suspect that, being Jewish, they'd anglicized the name to ease trade. They were pleasant people, had a well stocked shop, full of all the ex-military horrors we had become so used to wearing, as well as a lot of new work clothes for men, and stuff like oilskins and sou'westers for the local fishermen. As we entered Mr. Shields bounded towards us.

"Aha, Freda, Freda, how nice to see you. And look at boy Roy – *oi!* How he's grown! He's quite a young man now. No more short trousers, eh, son?"

Too damned right, I thought.

"So, Freda, what is it we're looking for this time?"

Mam worked through a list of pants, socks shoes and shirts for Alexander and Patrick, and after these items had piled up on the counter, it was my turn. Mrs. Shields had made a cup of tea and brought it to Mam, who was sitting on a chair.

"So, young Roy ma boy," said Mr. Shields, "what is he looking for?"

"Jeans," I said, flatly. He stroked his chin and nodded sagely.

"Ah, now. I've heard about these jeans things. These are the denims the American cowboys wear, am I right?"

I nodded.

"Levis," I said, realising how hopeless the word was.

"Mmm. We knew some Levis in Germany before the war. I wonder if they're related."

"They're called Levi Strauss," I said, "and they're in San Francisco."

Mrs Shields dipped a biscuit into her tea and looked wistfully into the middle distance.

"Ah, San Francisco. I'll bet they're doing good business there."

Mr. Shields went into the store room at the back of the shop and soon re-appeared carrying something made of denim – my heart raced. This looked very hopeful indeed. He spread them out on the counter.

"Now," he said, "these are not from Mr. Levi Strauss, but they're British and they're the nearest thing you'll get to those jeans. And they're denim." I went over to the counter and inspected them. The cardboard label proclaimed *Lybro Overalls*. Yes, they were denim, but the legs seemed as wide as a couple of power station cooling towers, and they had a joiner's ruler pocket down the side. Yet disappointed though I was, I felt instinctively that this was my only chance to strike out in the direction of James Dean. They were at least denim. They had pockets at the side and on the bum. I could adapt them; yes, yes, yes! This *could* work.

We left half an hour later with a couple of brown paper parcels. My booty was a pair of Lybro overalls, a lurid black and yellow lumberjack shirt and an unexpected delight – a pair of black baseball boots. Well, obviously they weren't real American baseball boots, just a glorified, ankle-height plimsoll with a circular rubber ankle patch, but they were groovy enough for me. Later that afternoon, I went into Woolworths and bought a packet of those two-pronged brass rivet-looking things which you use to clip documents together at the corner. I had seen through my scrutiny of the genuine Levis that they had rivets at the corner of the pockets. These would be my rivets.

The following Monday was to be our trip to Cleethorpes.

That Saturday night, when everyone was asleep, I put my plan into action. It was dark and sultry and I crept down stairs and went into the back yard. I took our tin bath from its hook on the wall, and began filling it from the standing tap. Soon the water was lapping over the top. I pulled on the Lybro overalls and lowered myself into the bath. I soon began to develop an even deeper admiration for James Dean. To think a man of his fame and good looks was prepared to suffer hypothermia, when he could have got someone else to shrink his pants for him. Maybe the weather and the water were milder in California. It wasn't a cold night down there by the fish dock either, but that water was something straight from the Arctic Circle. I sat there for thirty minutes patting the clammy denim to my legs. Eventually, I climbed out, fingers blue, teeth chattering, and hung the pants on the clothes line, emptied the bath and returned to bed.

The next morning there was a huge argument at first about the pants hanging in the yard. Yet I carefully explained what I was doing, how I had learned about this process, and the mood changed. I think Mam and Dad probably had a sneaking respect for my fledgling spirit of innovation. When the pants were finally dry, I repaired to my room and, using a penknife, punctured a little hole at the corner of each pocket and inserted a brass paperclip/stud. I was ready to rock and roll.

On the Monday morning, all togged up for our Cleethorpes expedition, which had three exciting elements – a trip across the Humber on the ferry to New Holland, then a steam train from New Holland to Cleethorpes, then the candy floss delight of the resort itself. It was about as exotic as holidays got.

Early in the morning we were standing by the bus stop on Hessle Road and I was examining the reflection of myself in Woolworth's shop window. I wasn't entirely happy. The 'jeans' didn't look all that 'Dean like' and the black and yellow shirt was two sizes too big. Yet, I thought, I looked different. I had made the effort. I continued to feel positive

until a Trinity House schoolmate, Bob Wardell, walked around the corner and ambled towards me. He stood a few feet away and looked me up and down, grinning from ear to ear. Out of earshot of Mam and Dad and the boys, he loomed in close and said in a low voice,
"What the *fuck* have you got on?"
I patted my legs.
"Jeans," I said, half proud.
"Well," said Bob, "you aught to give them back to Jean."
I was not amused.
"These are like … like James Dean," I offered, limply.
He stood back again and laughed.
"Well, mate," he said, "y'look a right *cunt!*"
To say that spoiled my day is an understatement. And by the time we were on the 9pm ferry home that night, it had been spoiled even more. The brass prongs of the paperclips inside my trousers and ripped into my flesh in several places and I could feel blood running down my legs. Was it Mr. Shields's fault? No. He did his best. This was the curse of Uncle Ken.

Leaving Boynton Street and Hessle Road was a much sadder occasion than departing from Nestor Grove six years earlier. All the friends I had there, the sense of community, the lively atmosphere, were ripped away overnight.
Yes, the house in Hedon was indeed a 'wooden bungalow'. It was three agricultural sheds knocked together. There was no lining to the inner walls, just the bare creosoted planks. It was a hell of a walk to the bus stop, and the winter was setting in. Dad, once again, was in his pioneering element. I was as happy as a mouse on a trap facing three hungry tomcats. What kind of Christmas would it be this year? I'd even lost my paper round now, and was back down to five bob a week. This meant I had to save up for three weeks to buy any records. Life at Trinity House School had taken several turns for the worse, and Mam and Dad had been sent a letter questioning the viability of my remaining there.

As we put the decorations up in our new wooden hovel that December, I was really worried about my future.

❖ ❖ ❖ ❖

15: THOUGH THE FROST WAS CRUEL

*'When he surrendered, Sitting Bull
knew the old life had gone forever.
He sang a new song:*

*A warrior
I have been,
Now
It is all over
A hard time
I have.'*

Dee Brown, *The American West* Simon & Schuster NY 1994

We could never quite work it out, my brothers and I. Was it 'Good King Wenceslas looked out' or was it 'Good King Wenceslas *last* looked out'? Looking back, I now realise it didn't matter. Those tunes, those carols, they filled the dark, sharp winter air with a promise of joy. Even 'We three Kings of Orien-tarr' followed by 'two in a bus and one in a car' could never interfere with the promise of Christmas day. We knew it was coming, and even if it proved to be an anti-climax, then the long days of December anticipation seemed worth it.

But on Christmas Eve, 1958, our family life had struggled to rise even a few degrees from the depth of poverty we'd felt since 1953. Our 'house', if one could call it such, Elm Bank, was really a trio of converted sheds, the size of three suburban garages, cobbled together to form a timber dwelling. It stood at the end of a long, cinder-topped un-adopted road. In the village of Hedon to the east of Hull, we were the last abode on this hotch-potch collection of similar wrecks known as Bond's Estate, the domiciles of numerous cash-strapped unfortunates like us who could neither afford to buy a home or had somehow dropped off the council housing list. That's not to say there were no 'proper' citizens living there. Some of the houses were paragons of scaled-down domestic pride, and most occupants made full use of their gardens for both food and decoration. Yet we were the rural poor, neither agricultural nor urban; just working people who had now chosen to live in the last place available before begging on the street. I had to ask myself; why did Mam and Dad keep doing this? It was one step above living in a caravan, yet caravans were usually better built than Elm Bank. Only one room, the living room, (shed one) was insulated against the elements by a lining of plasterboard and cheap wallpaper. It was heated by a rusting cast iron wood-burning stove. The bedrooms, (sheds two and three) still had the plain slatted timber of the agricultural prefabrications which they were – leaving nothing but just under a half inch of creosote-soaked pine between us and the vicious East Yorkshire winter. Behind the house stood a bank of tall poplar trees, and beyond them a meadow, at the end of which ran the Hull to Withernsea railway line. The bedroom occupied by myself and my two brothers, (shed three) was the nearest to the trees. At night, when the wind blew, the poplars creaked and moaned, their rustling leaves filtering the sinister moonlight through the cheap, rippled glass in the small, rickety widow frame. We knew the train timetable so well we hardly ever needed to look at a clock. At 9.30 pm the last locomotive towing two almost empty carriages would rumble and chuff across the bottom of the meadow on its way to the ersatz charm of Withernsea, a seaside town which, I'm sorry to say, really seemed like the last resort of any holidaymaker.

We were kept warm not only by several blankets, but with a counterpane on each bed courtesy of the Army and Navy Stores – three hefty ex-British Railways shunter's greatcoats, still equipped with their resplendent silver buttons. On those dark, merciless mornings of extreme winter coldness when we were shaken from our beds to get ready for basins of porridge and school, those railwaymen's greatcoats would be stiff with sheen of ice formed from the condensation which had risen from the slumbering bodies of three small boys. I was the oldest. By that December I had reached the mature ripeness of 14, and on Christmas Eve, although I didn't yet know it, I was about to stand on the first steps at the portal of manhood.

"We can't have another Christmas dinner like some we've had!" said Mam, shaking her head. Dad poked some more timber into the stove and puffed on his roll-up.

"And we won't, because I've got something sorted," he said.

Christmas Eve at Elm Bank in 1958 seemed to possess an air of promise. Dad was back in work. I continued to enjoy my weekly delight – the *New Musical Express*. Rock and Roll had arrived, and I thanked the Good Lord that here, we still had electricity, and we'd kept our radio and television set, and we had a Calor gas stove for cooking, although it was still the weekly tin bath. So, if our Yuletide feast wasn't to be Irish stew or even the luxury of chicken; I suspected rabbit pie; but perhaps I was wrong. What did Dad's cryptic proclamation mean? There was no such thing as turkey among the lumpen proletariat back then. Chicken was the ultimate luxury, and we even had a chicken coup, yet we'd killed so many of the poor devils for food that year that only three egg-laying hens and an indomitable, evil cockerel survived. Chicken was obviously off and no-one, even Dad, dare threaten Adolf the cockerel – he was a nasty piece of work and still the best alarm clock we had.

As the sharp, bitter darkness fell over the trees that Christmas Eve, spreading its icy fingers of hoarfrost across the surrounding scrubland, the bright moon arrived and the frozen, leaf-like filigree of frost crept across the window panes. My two younger brothers had been sent to bed, excited by thoughts of Father Christmas's imminent nocturnal visit. Yet for some reason, I was allowed to stay up. Was it because I was now some kind of 'second man' in the house? Did 14 now separate me from my receding childhood? I finished my *Musical Express* and watched some lame variety show on the TV. Then it happened. Dad switched the set off and, leaning in towards me in a conspiratorial fashion, filled me with a sense of horror as he outlined a mission he had obviously been planning for some time.

"Right, son. Christmas Eve. I've just been outside and lowered the saddle on my bike. I've checked the dynamo and the lights are working." He produced a piece of paper which bore an address scrawled in thick joiner's pencil.

"I want you to bike to Uncle Sid's on the Longhill Estate. That's the address. He's got something for us for our Christmas dinner." He handed me two pound notes.

"Give him this money, and tell him Stan wishes him a merry Christmas. Ride straight there and straight back, and don't stop for anybody. Right – now tell me what you've got to do?" I repeated the instructions. He looked at the clock.

"It'll take you about three quarters of an hour to get there, and the same to get back. It's quarter past nine now, so you ought to get back here by half past eleven."

"And don't forget to put your scarf on," said Mam, "and your gloves, and your balaclava." I hated that balaclava, but it was an arctic night, and ninety minutes of cycling lay ahead of me, a quite unexpected and highly dubious pleasure.

It seemed odd, pedalling for all I was worth along the long, straight run of the road between the village of Hedon and the twinkling lights of the oil refinery at Saltend. Odd because I was actually enjoying this. Dad, as an ex- Army sergeant, with 20 years in India and Europe under his belt, had shown his trust by giving me this important mission. That filled me with pride. What lay at the core of it was still a mystery, but as I slipped along through the crisp, cutting Christmas moonlight a new sense of purpose pushed my aching, cold knees into a blur.

It took me ten minutes of pedalling along past windows filled with shimmering Christmas trees on the Longhill Estate to find Uncle Sid's council house. I couldn't help wondering what it must be like in those solid brick homes; proper houses with proper rooms, tiled roofs, ceilings, fireplaces, boilers with immersion heaters – perhaps they even had baths. What must Christmas be like in these places? Maybe it was luxurious. We'd almost had it all, but now it was gone, yet again. I put it from my mind. I parked the bike and with wobbly legs ambled to the back door and knocked. Sid, a docker, was a wiry little man. Clad in a grubby vest and a pair of shiny gabardine trousers held up with string, he puffed on his briar pipe and eyed me up and down.

"Aha! It's lil'Roy, Stan's lad, eh?"

I nodded.

"Has he given you the money?"

I handed him the two pounds. I was very cold and I had hoped he might invite me in for a quick warm, but he simply instructed me to stand there by the door as he disappeared into the brick outhouse at the side of the tiny garden. I then heard a strange noise. A furious quacking sound, a fluttering, followed by a gargled squawk. This was repeated twice. Then, through the moonlight Sid appeared holding two fine and very dead ducks by their broken necks. He tied them together with a piece of string, walked over to the bike and slung them over the handlebars.

"Dad said Merry Christmas," I said.

"Tell him the same to him," replied Sid, "now get on that bike and ride like buggery all the way home. Tell your Mam about two and a half hours at gas mark 6. She'll love them birds."

This was all going remarkably well. Within half an hour

the lights of the refinery came into view again. The road was now a sheet of ice and every few yards I could feel the bike slipping slightly, yet I kept my balance and ploughed on. Soon, the village of Hedon appeared, its frosted roofs a blue-white in the moonlight, a living Christmas card. I leaned forward and felt the ducks. They were now frozen solid, the cold of their dead flesh penetrating through my gloves. I passed the closed off-licence, past the ladies' hairdresser's shop and the silent motor garage. The road was empty. No traffic. No cars. No pedestrians. Just a freezing, moonlit boy on an over-sized bicycle. Ahead stood the lofty façade of Saint Augustine's Church. Its tall, stained glass windows emitted pale golden light and as I drew closer, my breath shrouding my freezing face with a pale white cloud of bitter vapour, I could hear the choir singing. Of course, I thought – this must be for the Midnight Mass. It all seemed to fit together – this new sense of positivity, the ducks, my mission, and, as a bonus, those silvery voices were singing my mother's favourite carol. Then it happened.

The figure of the policeman seemed to come from nowhere. Like some sinister phantom from a Victorian penny dreadful, he stepped into the road a few yards ahead. He was wearing a heavy cape, and the beam from his lamp hit me in the eyes, temporarily dazzling me. I could see him only in silhouette as I drew closer. His hand was held up, open palm signalling me to stop. I gripped the brakes and drew to a skidding halt in the icy gutter. The sound of his hob-nailed boots, a comfort to those in the darkened, sleeping homes around us, was ominous to me. Yet that crunch along the tarmac was punctuated by the faint, angelic rise and fall of the Saint Augustine's choir.

'*Silent Night, Holy Night....*'

"Now then," the voice was a deep, gravelly and confident tenor, "and where d'you think *you're* off to my lad at this hour?"

'*All is calm, all is bright...*'

My heart was pounding.

"Er...I...I'm going home. I live up there – on the Bond's Estate."

"Mmm. Bond's Estate, eh? All the ruffians live there. Are you a ruffian?" I wasn't quite sure what a 'ruffian' was, but I didn't think I fitted the bill.

"No. I go to school."

He shone the torch on the ducks.

'Round yon Virgin Mother and Child
Holy Infant so tender and mild'

"And where did you get these beauties from then, son?"

I shivered.

"My Uncle Sid."

"And what does he do for a living?"

'Sleep in heavenly peace'

"He's...he's...he's a butcher. These ducks are for me Mam. For Christmas."

He lowered the beam of the torch. His vaporised breath mingled with mine and was sliced through by the moonlight as he leaned towards me. He had a big, round face with sharp, dark eyes, and sported a thick, well-groomed moustache. Our eyes seemed locked in an inseparable gaze; his one of inquisition, mine one of terror.

'Sleep in heavenly peace'

He fingered the ducks, weighed them in his huge hands, all the while staring at me. The choir seemed to grow louder, and I thought even then, in the presence of this strong arm of the law, that no matter what may happen, there was still something sadly beautiful in this sorry little tableau, something tragically Dickensian; a young boy, a policeman, a bicycle, two frozen ducks, an almost midnight, empty street and a church choir. A whole verse rang through the chill air as he stood there, pondering.

'Silent night, holy night!
Shepherds quake at the sight
Glories stream from heaven afar
Heavenly hosts sing Alleluia!'

I then saw something remarkable. His stern, inquiring visage appeared to melt into something more human. The eyes seemed softer. Then I realised that, like me, he too was listening to the music. He breathed in deeply, and to my utter amazement, a tear rolled down his cheek and vanished into the thick undergrowth of his moustache. One of those strong hands reached towards me and patted me on the shoulder.
"Aye....well. Alright son. You get yourself home and get warm. Off you go. Oh, and before I forget..."
I was about to pedal off.
"What?"
"Have a Merry Christmas."
As I rode away with all the speed I could muster, the faint tones of the choir subsided into the silvery night behind me.

'Christ, the Saviour is born
Christ, the Saviour is born'

My arrival in the warmth of Elm Bank's living room was a triumph, although Dad was concerned.
"Where the bloody *hell* have y'been, lad?"
I told him about the policeman.
"Christ. Y'didn't give him your address, did you?"
"No. But he wished me merry Christmas."
Dad produced a bottle of that favourite of all Hull's trawlermen, Red Duster Rum. He poured two small glasses. I was staggered when placed one into my cold hand and said
"'Knock it back, lad – you've earned it!"
As the searing liquid spread its warm fingers through my chest, it seemed as if my childhood had begun to slip away.
We sat around the spluttering stove plucking the ducks, ankle deep in feathers until the clock struck one. On some American Forces radio station they were playing *Good King Wenceslas*. I shall always remember that line....
"Though the frost was cruel..." Who was he? Police Constable Wenceslas? Did he really exist at all, or had I

simply experienced some adolescent Dickensian epiphany? I'll never know.

As I got ready for bed in the ice-bound bedroom, Dad's silhouette appeared in the doorway.

"Er...good job done, lad. Just do us a favour, though. When you go to East Park next time with your mates, stay away from the pond. There'll be a few ducks short this year...."

Upon my return to Trinity House in the snowy January of 1959, the writing was on the wall. After almost two years of trying to drum the principles of navigation and mathematics into my numb skull, I was now in the bottom three in my form for maths, and bright though I was at English, art and Dane's Dyke, those subjects didn't count. Even my reasonable ability in seamanship was not going to help. I was called into the office of the Headmaster. Mr. Eddon. He was inspecting a file on the desk in front of him, making little 'Hmmm...hmmm' noises as I stood to attention. He looked up.

"Hmmm... Bainton. I'd like to offer you some fudd for thought. Not all the boys who attend this school are destined for success. I've had a long talk with Mr. Campbell and he sees no future for you in the Merchant Navy as an officer. I think it would be good if you asked your parents to come and see us. Will you do that?"

I nodded nervously and was duly dismissed.

Mam turned up at school after our dinner break on the last Friday in January. Miss Bird, the school secretary, brought her a chair and we sat waiting in the corridor. We were eventually joined by my maths and navigation master. Jock Campbell. He was remarkably polite, considering his penchant for sarcasm.

"Your son, Mrs. Bainton, could stay here for another year and take his exams, but he's 16 in April, and I think, frankly, he'd be better off finding a job. If he ever gets anywhere near a ship's chart room it'll be women and children first. I'm not saying he couldn't go to sea – indeed, he'd probably make a fine saloon steward or even a deckhand, but he isn't officer material."

Mam looked crestfallen. "I see. Is there any point in his staying?"

"Not really. He's not a bad lad, so we're not expelling him, but," he turned to face me, "I don't think you're happy here, Roy, are you?"

"No," I replied, glumly, "I'm not."

I was amazed. I could never have imagined he was capable of such sensitivity. Perhaps he only reserved it for boys he wanted chucking out. Campbell shook hands with my mother, then, to my surprise, with me, and as he walked away, he looked back at me and winked. It seemed a curious gesture.

There were no recriminations at home. Mam and Dad were pretty cool about it all. I had more chance of being Crazy Horse than I'd ever have at being Captain Cook.

The following week Mam and I went into town to the Baker Street youth employment and careers offices off Albion Street. The friendly careers man went through several apprenticeship options. Plumber? Electrician? Joiner? Plasterer? Bricklayer? I recoiled in dismay. Then Mam said to him

"Well, his teacher at Trinity House did say he could still go into the Merchant Navy."

The careers officer smiled broadly.

"Oh, well - why didn't you *say*? He could take a course at the Sea Training School at Gravesend and as he's sixteen in April, if he qualifies, he could be at sea in three months time." And so we filled in the forms. I was to do a six week catering course at Gravesend to learn to become a ship's steward. The prospect was scary, but deep down it was more exciting than becoming a plumber. At least I'd get away somewhere. Maybe even America.

As Mam and I sat in silence on the bus into Hull in the first week of February an icy, wind-lashed sleet smashed against the windows like machine gun bullets. I thought of the time when Crazy Horse finally arrived at Fort Robinson, Nebraska in September 1877, knowing his years of struggle and resistance were behind him, and that he would have to adapt to the ways of the white man. This was my Fort Robinson. If there was a pivotal moment I could mark as the end of childhood, then that was the day. I had my Dad's ex-army kitbag stuffed with clothes, mainly socks and underwear, a couple of shirts clean handkerchiefs, a soap bag and some spare shoes. I'd been told that upon arrival at Gravesend we would be issued with the Sea Training School's official uniform. Damn, I thought. Another bloody uniform.

Two days before a letter had arrived containing a British Railways travel warrant to get me from Hull to King's Cross, then via Charing Cross to Gravesend. At that time the furthest I had ever been was Cleethorpes, Halifax and Mytholmroyd. Now I was bound for London. At Paragon Station Mam bought a platform ticket to see me off. The sleety rain seemed to force itself horizontally beneath the massive Victorian station roof, making the platform wet and slippery. We hugged and kissed, she handed me a large brown paper bag containing sandwiches and a pork pie, the ultimate comestible comfort for the reluctant traveller, and I climbed aboard the Third Class carriage and sat by the window. I had a lump in my throat as I stared at my poor Mother through the window. Why were we always condemned to be so poor, so shabby? Standing there on the platform in her old coat and headscarf, clutching her shopping bag, her eyes red with tears, she smiled back at me. What lay ahead for us was unprecedented; I was to be away from home in a new, uncertain environment for six whole weeks. That was the length of school holidays in the summer, to quote Wordsworth, 'sweet childish days, that were as long as twenty days are now', when six weeks seemed like a golden eternity.

The guard blew his whistle and the steam locomotive huffed and puffed into action. As we gathered speed, I stood by the compartment window in tears, waving as Mam broke into a semi-sprint along the platform, trying to hang on to the sight of her son for as long as possible. To my horror, she slipped and fell her full length onto the wet surface. I rolled down the window and put my head out as the train picked up speed, and to my relief watched a friendly porter picking her up to her feet. Then the vision receded and I was gone.

My old life had vanished for ever. Within a few weeks, after the month and a half of stern discipline and hard work at Gravesend, on my 16th birthday on April 1st, I would be climbing the gangway to board my first ship. I was no longer Crazy Horse, Dan Dare, James Dean or Elvis. I was about to be forcibly immersed into the world of men, where innocence has no currency.

16: DEATH OF A HERO

'It is to the interest of the commonwealth of mankind that there should be some one who is unconquered, some one against whom fortune has no power.'
Seneca (4 B.C. – A.D. 65)

I think those historians who refer to Crazy Horse's capitulation as 'surrender' are wrong. Such a hero cannot exist in bondage; somehow, his only ultimate freedom would be death. As F. Scott Fitzgerald wrote; 'Show me a hero and I will write you a tragedy'.

Even in that bitter, blizzard winter of 1976-7, when chiefs Spotted Tail and Red Cloud had definitely surrendered and brought their people into the reservations, Crazy Horse, relentlessly pursued by General Nelson Miles's merciless infantry, held out. With all their shells, armour and military prowess, the U.S. Army had not 'tamed' the Indians yet. Sitting Bull had gone with his band to Canada, where 'Great Grandmother', our own Queen Victoria, would allow him to live in peace. His only mistake would be to return to America. And parallel to his struggle with Crazy Horse, General George Crook was in the midst of another war with the Nez Perce, led by the indomitable Chief Joseph, and he had several more years of struggle ahead with Geronimo.

The snow forced Miles and his men back to base, but Crazy Horse's Sioux band had eluded him. To the Generals, like Miles, Crook and others, Tsunke Witco remained the strategic prize they most desired, because his surrender to one of them would assure their military glory. Yet when the time came, Crazy Horse would sit down not with a three star general, but with a more thoughtful and understanding young Lieutenant, Philo Clark.

Crazy Horse was known to the Oglala Sioux as their 'Strange Man', because of his remarkable spiritual nature and sense of vision. He would often disappear into the hills for days to commune with the Great Spirit. Over a decade before he thrashed Custer at Little Big Horn he had a vision of how he might die. He knew that he could ride into battle as a leader and that bullets would somehow miss him. He was once wounded by an arrow in the leg aimed by a U.S. Army Crow scout, but in general he had been remarkably lucky. Yet the vision he had whilst still a young brave was that he might one day die if one of his own people held his arms so that he could not fight.

General George Crook, known to the Indians as 'Three Stars' had sent a promise to Crazy Horse that he could have his own agency, and therefore would not have to live on his uncle Spotted Tail's reservation or Red Cloud's. What Crazy Horse did not know, was that Crook had secret plans to send the Chief and his band first to Omaha and then to exile on the Dry Tortugas, a group of barren islands off the Florida Keys. A more severe and cruel fate for a man of the wide open plains could not be imagined. Crook also promised that Crazy Horse's people would be allowed to hunt buffalo again. Crook was essentially a good man and a brilliant soldier, but as with all the deals he voiced on behalf of Washington, these 'promises' were nothing but lies.

When Crazy Horse arrived at Fort Robinson, the base commanded by General Bradley, on May 9th 1977, he led a column of 900 Sioux followed by 2,000 ponies. As this 2-mile long parade passed among the Sioux already living there, the Indians all united and began to sing their victory song. This, as one officer commented, was no surrender; it was a triumphal march. Over the next few days, they would be forced to surrender their guns and horses, but based on Crook's promises, they felt optimistic that soon they would get their own reservation on Beaver Creek, and return to the buffalo hunt.

Yet things went wrong from the start. Without doubt, Crazy Horse was the hero of his people, and the young braves held him in high esteem. It was already common knowledge that Spotted Tail's people were jealous of Red Cloud's band, but now, the greatest Sioux of all had entered the equation. The old chiefs began to wonder if the whites might make this younger upstart the chief of them all. Soon, the bitter acid of deceit, backbiting and betrayal would lead to tragedy. A lone figure, apart from his family, Crazy Horse had few close friends. They included He Dog, and the seven-foot-tall Minniconjou Lakota warrior Touch the Clouds. After the years of mistrust, lies, squabbling, war and broken treaties, Crazy Horse had entered a world where he felt he could trust no-one.

Despite the blandishments and pleas heaped upon him by the U.S. officials to persuade him to go to Washington, Crazy Horse resolutely refused. He knew he would be displayed in front of the President as a war trophy, and he made his own deal – I'll go – but give us our reservation first. Then in July, Crook was looking for assistance in his bitter war with the Nez Perce. Some Sioux and Cheyenne were willing to go to Crook's aid and fight, but Crazy Horse regarded the request as sheer stupidity. First, he said, you take our horses and guns and we come to live with you in peace; now you want us to go to war again – against other Indians?

Yet day by day the Army kept up the pressure, whilst in the background, evil rumours and lies were spread by an Indian called Woman's Dress that Crazy Horse had secret plans of his own to go back on the warpath. In a meeting with the Army Crazy Horse finally lost his patience. He agreed he would go and fight the Nez Perce, but the interpreter, a scout named Frank Grouard, for some odd reason, deliberately misinterpreted his words. What Crazy Horse actually said was;

"Yes, I will go and fight the Nez Perce, but if I do, I will fight until every last Nez Perce is killed." Grouard translated this as *until every last white man* is killed. This cruel misrepresentation created a massive panic at Fort Robinson.

General Crook was outraged. Yet when he sent Indian Policemen to Crazy Horse's lodge to arrest him, he wasn't there. He had travelled 40 miles that day to see his wife, Black Shawl, who was being treated for tuberculosis at the agency of his uncle, Spotted Tail. He was happy she was being well cared for, but he soon discovered that Grouard's faulty translation had now placed him in great danger. Spotted Tail's Agent, Jesse Lee, advised him that it was best to go back to Fort Robinson and put things right with the command there.

Confident that he could explain things to General Bradley, he decided to return to Fort Robinson. On the return journey he was met by a heavily armed column of blue-coated Indian soldiers, who escorted him back to the fort and into the parade ground, where around a thousand angry Indians had gathered.

Crazy Horse dismounted, retrieved a red blanket from his horse and carried it over his arm. Flanked by Indian policemen, he made his way to General Bradley's office. But Bradley refused to see him. He wanted to tell the General that he had no plot against Crook, nor any intention of killing white people again. However, Bradley's stark message was that Crazy Horse was under arrest and should be taken to the fort's jail – the guard house. As he was being led away, his old 7-foot friend Touch the Clouds came forward. Then, to Crazy Horse's surprise, another old comrade in arms, Little Big Man, dashed up and gripped him by the elbows. He was steered through a doorway into a stinking building with barred windows. To the free-roving Sioux, the idea of a jail or prison did not exist. But Crazy Horse knew what this building was, with its tragic occupants, white deserters shackled with balls and chains.

He turned sharply on his heels and dashed back through the door, but Little Big Man was now grabbing him by his arms to hold him back. Yet from under the blanket, the ever alert Crazy Horse pulled a knife and slashed at Little Big Man's wrist. Shocked, Little Big man let go his grip.

Then the voices – both English and Lakota, cut through the dusty air.

"Shoot him! Shoot him! Stab the son of a bitch!" Guns were cocked. An Irish Private, one William Gentles, a native of County Tyrone, leapt forward and stabbed Crazy Horse twice in the kidneys. Bleeding profusely, he fell to the ground. Although Bradley still insisted that, wounded or not, he should be consigned to the guard house, Touch the Clouds pleaded with him and eventually the general allowed the dying chief to be taken into the adjutant's office. The towering, mighty warrior carried his wounded friend in, and was about to place him in a cot, but Crazy Horse requested that they lay him on the floor.

Doctor Valentine McGillycuddy, the camp surgeon who had been treating Black Shawl for her tuberculosis, administered morphine to soothe Crazy Horse's pain. As it grew dark, he dozed a while, until by the light of a smoking oil lamp, he opened his eyes. His distraught father, Worm, had arrived.

"Son, I am here," said his father.

Crazy Horse was fading fast.

"Father, it is no good for the people to depend on me any longer - I am bad hurt."

Crazy Horse died on the floor at 11:30 pm. He was 36 years old. Touch the Clouds pulled the red blanket over him.

"This is the lodge of Crazy Horse," he said.

His parents, overcome with grief, took the body away to the Black Hills and the secret of where he is buried died with them.

Although, as a young sailor, the Merchant Navy took me to the USA, to most of the ports down the eastern seaboard from Boston, New York and all the way to Charleston, South Carolina, I have never been to Nebraska or South Dakota. I have not seen the Black Hills, or stood in the shadow of that massive work-in-progress, the Crazy Horse monument on Thunder Mountain. Chances are now, as I reach the age of 68, with the rigours of post-9/11 terrorism paranoia making long-distance flying a complicated trial rather than a pleasure, perhaps I never will.
The rolling plains and the Black Hills are destined to remain as they existed in my childhood: glorious vistas in my wild imagination.

There are several places claimed to be the burial plot of Tsunke Witco. Yet he is in the spirit world, where he is free, where the buffalo hunt goes on and his people still roam in their eternal liberty. Yet if there are many places he might rest, then one of them is in my heart. In my panoply of other heroes, gathered one by one through each decade of my life, he still rides his pony through them all, supreme and unchallenged.

He was with me on that golf course when I was 8 years old; he is with me today. To General Miles, he was 'the embodiment of ferocity'. To me, his courageous life, his love for freedom and his people will always be an inspiration. As Black Elk so astutely observed;
'It does not matter where his body lies,
for it is grass; but where his spirit is, it will be good to be'

The End